D0054062

# Dogs

*Photographs by Susanne Page*

*Illustrations by Jake Page*

⊙ Smithsonian Books

Collins
An Imprint of HarperCollins Publishers

# Dogs

## A NATURAL HISTORY

### Jake Page

Preface by Stanley Coren

HarperCollins books may be purchased for educational, business, or sales promotional use. For information, please write: Special Markets Department, HarperCollins Publishers Inc., 10 East 53rd Street, New York, NY 10022.

All photographs appearing within the text © Susanne Page.

All illustrations appearing within the text © Jake Page.

FIRST EDITION

*Designed by Chris Welch*

**Library of Congress Cataloging-In-Publication Data**

Page, Jake.

    Dogs : a natural history / Jake Page ; photographs by Susanne Page ; illustrations by Jake Page.

       p. cm.

    Includes bibliographical references and index.

    ISBN 978-0-06-113259-9

    1. Dogs.   I. Title.

SF426.P317   2007

636.7—dc22

          2007017059

07  08  09  10  11  wbc/qw  10 9 8 7 6 5 4 3 2 1

For Susanne

# CONTENTS

# Part Three: The Dog's World

# Appendixes

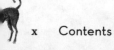

Old Nell (R.I.P.) and Curry (age twelve weeks)

# PREFACE

Where do dogs come from? How did they form their association with humans? Can dogs really think? All of these questions have been asked millions of times over eons of time. There have been many attempts to answer them. One which I heard when I was younger came from a preacher whose ministry was a small rural church in West Virginia.

The story goes that when Adam and Eve had defied God by eating the apple from the forbidden tree, God drove them from the Garden of Eden. He placed an angel at the gate to bar their return to Paradise and he placed a pack of beasts there as well, to serve as guards which would enforce the ban. These beasts were great wolf-like animals with strong jaws and the ability to run very fast. They already had knowledge of humans since they had observed and interacted with them when all creatures lived together peacefully in the garden. However, there was dissention in the pack when they were given their new task. Some, who had been resentful of the special treatment that humans received from God, were pleased at their new job. They would gladly hurt any person because their jealousy had made them vengeful. Others had grown fond of the humans, feeling that there was still a spark of the divine in them. These worried about the safety of such fragile beings in the wild and dangerous world outside of Paradise. It was this second group who decided that they would go with Adam and Eve, to keep them company, to guard their safety, and to work with them to help them prosper.

When God looked down and saw that some of his pack of guardians had abandoned their post to travel with the humans he became angry.

"Why do you not perform the task I asked of you?" he roared.

The leader of this group, an animal named Keleb, spoke up. "My Lord, if you had wanted these people to die you would have slain them in the garden. Instead you drove them out and charged us with the task of keeping them from ever returning. We will try to keep them alive as seems to be your will, and we will also keep them from trying to come back. We will do this working with them, by being their work mates and soul companions. If they feel that they can survive and prosper on their own, then perhaps they can try to build their own version of a Garden of Eden. Knowing that this can be done will keep them from attacking the gates of Paradise. Knowing the amount of labor that is required will also teach them the value of what they have lost by disobeying you."

God smiled at Keleb's words and said, "This is a wise and noble thing that you are doing. As a reward I will put in the hearts and minds of humans a special place that can be filled with love and affection for your kind and the generations that follow you."

It is said that the animals who stayed to guard the gates were wolves and those who accompanied man into the wilderness became dogs. Dogs still work with and guard humans because it is a contract made with God. Humans, in turn, love dogs, because without a love of dogs there would be an empty place in their hearts and minds.

In this book, you will find a very different history of the origin of dogs. Jake Page does paint a beginning that starts with a wide variety of wild canines, and in a way he finds that there were some who remained wolves and some who chose to become dogs. There are, however, no angels in his treatment, but rather the action of evolution, natural selection, DNA, and human manipulation. This is not, however, a cold scientific history, but rather a transformation of one animal species into another that is helped along by humans, and is ultimately a benefit for both species.

Once he has told you how dogs came to be, he goes on to tell you how dogs perceive the world around them, how they think and solve problems, and how they communicate with people and other dogs. In the process you will learn that while dogs, as a species, have been shaped by evolution and the intervention of people, each individual dog is also shaped by its own history, which includes its history of interactions with humans. Along the way you will get a very practical glimpse of how such things come about when Jake Page describes the lives, histories and behaviors of his own dogs—a half-dozen animals who fill those empty spaces in his heart and mind.

Stanley Coren

JUNO

# AUTHOR'S NOTE

**M**uch of what I have found myself doing for the past three-plus decades is the fault of my wife Susanne. It is she who introduced me to the American Southwest and actual American Indians in the form of the Hopis and Navajos. She also introduced me to a prothonatory warbler in a bush on the C & O Canal outside of Washington, D.C., leading to a continuing interest in birds which are, happily, always an important part of wherever I go. It was Susanne who saw to it that we kept a Polish hen and her chick in our bathroom for a long period, created four (count 'em) koi ponds at a house that sat close to the desert, and until recently had a bearded dragon living on the dining room table. Also, if it were not for Susanne, I doubt that my household would include six dogs.

Since they will make appearances in the course of this book, both in the text and in Susanne's photographs, I introduce them herewith, in order of seniority:

* * *

*Amelia*, a female. Rescued from the pound in Espanola, New Mexico, she has huge, rounded, erect ears that begged for the name Amelia Earhart. A large black dog with a tendency to the beaminess of a Labrador retriever, she apparently (and improbably) has some fairly recent Corgi blood, explaining the size and shape of her ears. How a Lab-sized dog and a diminutive Corgi could have pulled off such a feat lies beyond my imagination. Low-slung on legs that are disproportionately short for her size (more Corgi?), she is the canine equivalent of a low-rider, which is appropriate enough, what with Espanola being a world-class low-rider capital.

Amelia, now some thirteen years old, has a white face and arthritis. She is extremely good-natured, and patient with kids who happily trample her. Amelia occasionally challenges the youngest dog, a male, to play with her, which sadly he seems puzzled by at best. And every now and then she exercises a minimal kind of dominance over the young male.

*Curry*, a male. The name is short for Coeur de Lion, or lionhearted, a prospective name that seemed necessary. A Rez dog from a Navajo camp, he was one of three pups born to a Navajo sheep dog who disappeared, abandoning them to live in the sheep pen. Curry and his two siblings were used as toys by the Navajo children—pulled, thrown, and generally abused until they were big enough to run away. We fetched Curry from an underground den and he spent his first month in our house under the bed.

For the next eight years he would not let anyone but us touch him. Then a very young granddaughter, over a period of about an hour, got him completely over these fears. He is extremely elegant looking, a slender, long-legged, and long-necked dog with a hint of greyhound, and Doberman coloring. He sits erect, head high, and looks a bit like the Egyptian dog-god Anubis.

*Teacup*, a female. Named by a (different) granddaughter who was wearing a nightgown with cups and saucers on it at the time. Teacup is another Rez dog. Her mother was a feral dog on the Hopi reservation, rescued by a young Hopi woman who subsequently married a man from the Cochiti Pueblo, who had a large retriever-ish male. The young woman's uncle, a dear friend of ours, insisted that we take one of the puppies. They were all tiny, dun-colored, scrawny with little rat tails curled tightly over their backs—ugly as sin and not the sort of dog one would immediately cotton to.

A canine version of the ugly duckling, Teacup grew into a good-sized and handsome dog with the erect ears and dark face of German shepherd but with a full brushy tail that curves upward. She has a beautiful tan coat the texture of cashmere. Extremely intelligent, nervous, and in general fearful of new presences as well as the sound of thunder, she has invented several unique rituals for herself, and is loquacious to a fault. (It is interesting to note that Hopis tend to be very talkative while Navajos, and particularly Navajo males, tend to be quiet, as does Curry.)

*Juno*, a female. Susanne had longed for an Australian shepherd over the years and we heard about a rancher who had bred an obedience-champion Australian shepherd with an obedience-champion Australian Cattle Dog (or Blue heeler) with a view to creating the perfect ranch dog. Well aware that we had plenty of dogs already, we went to look and unsurprisingly took home the puppy who insisted on being with us. She became Juno, midsized, mostly black but tricolored with a snowy white tip on her tail and expressive erect ears.

Now five years old, Juno tolerates the other dogs, often by simply leaving their company altogether for another room. It is clear that she does not really think she is a mere dog like the others. She sits on a haunch with her hind legs stretched out to the side like a human, and often rolls her eyes heavenward, as if to say, "Look at those nitwits."

When she is on a walk and in full chase of a rabbit or duck, all Susanne has to say is her name and she spins around in full stride and returns immediately to Susanne's side, meaning that perhaps obedience has a genetic component.

Juno is very earnest, and takes her self-appointed job of watching over us with great seriousness. For example, whenever I emit the sort of snort associated with sleep apnea, I will be awakened by being pawed by Juno, who will have taken up a position sitting by my head.

*Jupiter*, a male. A daughter insisted that we take one of two "miniature" Australian shepherds she had acquired and we wound up with Jupiter, a big name for the smallest member of our canine solar system. Tri-colored and long-haired (except in the summer when he gets shaved), he is mostly shiny black with a luxurious white ruff on his chest, cinnamon legs, and white feet. He is ever cheerful. Treated (by me) as a lap dog when he was tiny, he retains the desire to lie on my chest if I lie on a sofa, and he has a nearly fanatic desire to lick people that is hard to break him of. (His brother was the same in this regard. Unfortunately, the brother got run over.)

One day when he was four, Jupiter began losing his balance and we soon discovered that he had experienced what pet neurologist Steve Colter called a vascular event in the right side of his brain. It is early in life for something like this to happen. Jupiter has since regained his balance, but occasionally jerks his head to the right, or spins tightly to the right—all involuntarily. At first he was confused to find himself looking back over his shoulder, but he has adjusted to it and remains cheerful and full of fun.

*Ding*, a male. One day Susanne and I and several of the dogs were walking along an irrigation ditch in New Mexico when Jupiter ran off down a road, returning with a very small gray puppy following him. Jupiter crossed a bridge and joined us while the gray puppy leaped into the ditch, swam across, and scrambled up the bank, attaching himself to my right foot where he remained until we got home. He appeared to be about eight weeks old and his toenails were abraded down to nubbins. He had evidently come a long way.

He simply adopted us. He is mostly if not wholly Blue heeler, with a dramatic black patch over one eye and pointed, erect ears. For some reason he reminded me of the Australian dog, the Dingo, hence the name. (I found out later that Blue heelers were bred by mixing Dingo genes with those of some domesticated breeds.)

He is adept at getting his own way, typically first when the dogs burst out the door in a frantic stampede. (We have since handled the stampede by putting in a dog door which Ding was typically first to master.) Oddly expressionless, he sometimes reminds me of a Spielberg dinosaur. Smoothly furred, with a long tail that is often wagging, Ding is an admirable athlete and spends a lot of time patrolling the fence around our two acres. Once he spotted a big coyote in our yard and ran it off without a moment's hesitation.

In all, they are a pretty peaceable lot, much more so than one would expect in, say, a household of six human siblings. For the most part, like the dogs Elizabeth Marshall Thomas wrote about in *The Hidden Life of Dogs*, they trained themselves, although this is frowned upon by every known member of what is called the dog industry. Even so, most of the time any one of them will come immediately upon being called, which is all we really require of them outside of reasonably consistent house training. We spend a small fortune on dog food, of course, and veterinarians, and longingly if languidly seek a market for dog hair.

# Dogs

JUPITER, JUNO, AND TEACUP

*Introduction*

# On Natural History

On many occasions when all six of our dogs are present in the room, I have wondered how each could be so different—in appearance, personality, and style. Who are these guys? What's on their minds? How did they get that way? And when? These questions led me to that grand old study called natural history. How do these six stack up against what is known about dogs in general—in terms of things like smarts? Are they real animals or are they, in some domesticated, tamed way, artifacts?

I looked around for a book straightforwardly on the natural history of dogs, not how to train a dog or what distinguishes the various dog breeds. Just their natural history. I had spent a lot of time (as an editor) in natural history museums in New York and Washington, D.C., so I thought I might be up for such a task. So this book is the result, but first here are some thoughts on that grand old study: natural history.

Start then with a collection of creatures who all have forty-two teeth, and another collection who all have thirty. That, plus a few other details, was enough for Carolus Linnaeus who, in the 1750s, set out to name and catalogue all living things in the name of science. The second group could all be lumped together and known as cats or felids or (even more scientifically) Felidae. The first group, the one with the forty-two teeth, could be considered separate from the cats and called dogs, or canids or Canidae. (In scientific circles, Canidae is pronounced *can-i-dee*, even though the ancient Romans pronounced *dae* as *dye*, but never mind.)

Sorting out animals (and plants, of course) in this manner is called taxonomy, or systematics. It involves figuring out the extent of relatedness of animals and animal groups and giving them the two Latinate names that most of us find so hard to remember much less pronounce. So we have *Canis lupus* which means literally Dog wolf, and *Canis familiaris*, that is Dog domesticated. Linnaeus invented this two-part, or binomial, system for naming animals and plants. It lets someone who can remember all the names place a creature on the great genealogical tree of life on this planet. It was a remarkable idea at the time and it still works tolerably well (though I will have a few admonitory comments on some of the binomial names attached to certain canids).

Besides mounting exhibitions, taxonomy is the business that museums of natural history have long concerned themselves with, and most of them are still so engaged some of the time, as are a few university biology departments. So far taxonomists have identified and named some 1,750,000 species, from the tiniest one-celled marine creatures to the world's largest animal, the blue whale. This is an impressive record for work that began only about 250 years ago and has never been pursued by more than a few thousand people at any given time. Yet there are anywhere from thirteen to thirty million more species out there, it is estimated, that have never been seen, much less identified. Never mind that most of these millions of unknowns are insects and things like yeasts and bacteria. It is still an astonishing number when you think of how much of the planet human beings have redesigned for their own purposes. It has been estimated, for example, that well over half of all the photosynthesis that takes place on the Earth's landforms now produces agricultural plants for humans (and pets and gas tanks).

Thousands of new species are discovered each year. Most are found in previously inaccessible places, like the high atmosphere, deep in soils, in the ocean and around hot vents on the ocean floors, in the canopies of rain forests, and even within animals themselves. Recently some 200 species of yeast have been found inhabiting the gut of certain beetles, and these yeasts are not likely to ever appear in the *New York Times*. But biologists do come across a surprising number of more conspicuous animals and plants that were either thought to be extinct or were never before seen or imagined.

The Woolemi pine tree was presumed to have gone extinct in its native Australia two million years ago, only to be found still clinging to the planet there in 1994. In 2005, a whole new family of rodents came to light in Laos—the kha-nyou, as it is known by the locals, or otherwise and unpoetically the Laotian rock rat—who supposedly had been extinct for eleven million years. A new South American monkey received its binomial monicker in 2005. The scientist who found it auctioned off the right to name it, the proceeds going to help preserve its habitat. It is the only mammal ever named for a gambling casino: *Callicebus aureipalatii*, the Golden Palace titi. And in 2005 a new wild dog species turned up in Borneo—a new fox. Caught on film from a mounted camera in one of the island's national parks, the fox has a reddish coat, a bushy tail, and extended rear legs that suggest that it might be partly arboreal. In the following year, 2006, scientists announced the discovery of more than fifty new species of plants and animals in Borneo.

Beginning in the 1950s with major discoveries like the double-helix structure of DNA, natural history and taxonomy began to be perceived as pretty old-fashioned and staid—not at all a groovy scientific realm. And indeed the shiny hi-tech world of molecular biology has taken us deep into the arenas of the genes and viruses, and the brave new world of clones and chimeras (this last being combinations of two different animals). The biology of very small parts of living things has also refined the old eye- and microscope-based Linnean practice of taxonomy by comparing such things as DNA to check on the degree of relatedness of creatures.

I take all this relatively wonderful and explosive science as being new additions to the capacious old field of natural history. It tells us, for example, that there is hardly any difference in the DNA of wolves and every breed of domesticated dog on the planet. How can that be? How is it that a seventy-pound wolf, a one hundred and eighty-pound mastiff and a three-pound Chihuahua have the same genes? Could the DNA experts be confused?

And what is a species anyway? It is usually described as a group of animals (or plants) that can successfully breed with one another but cannot breed with other closely related animals. The classic example is the horse and donkey who, if mated, produce a mule, which is a sterile animal who cannot produce progeny. But even before DNA studies of dogs and wolves came along, the members of the genus *Canis* were something of a taxonomic embarrassment. Wolves, coyotes, jackals, and domestic dogs all have their separate binomial species names. But they all can and occasionally do interbreed and create perfectly successful and fecund hybrids. In fact, defining a species is a fairly abstract and technical matter that we needn't bother with.

Natural history is impelled by nothing less than a reasonable interest in learning who your neighbors are and what they might require of you, in addition to what, if anything, they might do for you. For example, can this plant promote human health? Can the genetic code of a dog be used in the fight against diabetes? Outside of the microscopic creatures we carry around in and on our bodies, we have no closer, more intimately familiar nonhuman animal neighbors than dogs, and the past few decades have seen a virtual explosion of research in veterinary schools and some university biology departments on the evolution and biology of these animals.

Vets, for example, have recently concentrated a great deal more brainpower on the behavior of dogs, the better to understand and serve them medically. Scientists have spelled out the genetic code (DNA) of dogs along with humans and a few other animals. Since we share a lot of congenital diseases with dogs and about 75 percent of our genes, getting such a close view of dogs will probably be beneficial to us all. In fact, we know a great deal more about our dogs now than we did even a few years ago. Who, ten years ago, would have imagined that dogs laugh?

In some simple ways, our dogs train us. But in practically

every way we control them, and they rely almost wholly on us for their quality of life. For that reason alone it behooves us to know them as thoroughly and as intimately as we can—to know who they are, how they got that way, and how they perceive their world.

*Part One*

# THE LIMITS OF DOGDOM

*The lineage of dogs, the Canidae, came about as long-legged carnivores given to chasing prey animals across long distances in mostly open country. How much variation on that ground plan is possible?*

AMELIA (EARHART)

## Chapter One

# Origins and Oddballs

If someone asked you where domestic dogs came from, the chances are you would say wolves, and you would be correct. Over the years scientists have argued about this question, saying maybe some came from coyotes or jackals, but these days it is clear that dogs derived exclusively from wolves, and almost surely from wolves who inhabited the huge Eurasian continent. The process of domestication could have taken place anywhere from some 15,000 years to more than 100,000 years ago, depending on which scientists you pay most attention to—geneticists or archaeologists—but never mind that for now. We'll get to it in a later chapter.

Let's start with wolves. First, where did they come from? That leads us to a time sixty or so million years ago, after the dinosaurs had vanished, leaving the field to the humble mammals. Some of these were ferret- and shrew-sized mammals with lithe bodies and long tails. Called miacids, they were arboreal creatures, and from them arose all of the meat-eating mammals called carnivores. Some of the miacids gave rise to the lineage represented today by the cats, hyenas, civets, and mongooses.

Some miacids gave rise to a lineage called Caniformia—which is to say, dog-related: dogs, raccoons, bears, sea lions, seals, walruses and weasels. And the first of these creatures to arise was called Hesperocyon (which means,

*Miacid*

approximately, dog of the evening). They were for the most part about the size of small foxes, with supple bodies, long tails, and fairly short muzzles. They walked on their toes (like modern dogs) and so they are considered the first actual canids. In addition, they were good tree climbers. (I should point out that what you have here in this brief evolutionary tale is the equivalent of a few still photographs taken out of a very long, and very complicated movie.)

One of these early canids was *Cynodictis*, which lived in the forests of North America some forty million years ago. It had several features that turned out to be characteristic of most dog-like animals ever thereafter: longer legs, a particularly bony growth in the ear called the auditory bulla (which you may now forget about), and a bigger braincase than its ancestors. Also, it had scissor-like

*Cynodictis*

cheek teeth called carnassial teeth for shearing and chewing meat, a telltale sign of a meat eater be it a dog or a cat or any other carnivore.

As long as forty million years ago, the canids were already on their way to becoming long-distance runners suited to pursuing game over open ground, exhausting their prey the way wolves do, scissoring out big chunks of meat and bolting them down. Over the millions of years the legs would grow longer, the feet longer and more compact, the tail shorter. Five spreading toes would turn into the four compact toes (plus the dew claw) adapted to running fast over considerable distance. They ran on their toes only, what scientists call digitigrade. The basic shape and pattern and number (forty-two) of the teeth would remain similar. The essential pattern of today's dog, in other words, was established.

## Digitigradience

I believe I have made this word up. It means the condition of walking on one's toes, which is what most modern predators do and, in the case of dinosaurs, did. Birds walk on their toes, as do cats, hippos, and, of course, dogs. The familiar term, dogleg, is a result of digitigradience: the bones that correspond to the rest of a typical foot are held off the ground, sloping rearward with the ankle and foreleg angled forward from the (nonexistent) heel.

Animals who plant their entire foot on the ground are called plantigrade, and they include bears, squirrels, mice, and humans. Unguligrade refers to ungulates, the name for hoofed animals like horses, goats, antelopes, and deer. For example, in the case of the horse, the claw of the middle toe evolved into a single toe (the others becoming mere slivers), which became the hoof.

My word digitigradience also suggests a continuum, variation. Our dog Amelia walks on her toes but they spread out a lot, to the extent that you might be forgiven for thinking she was plantigrade. On the other hand, Ding, the Australian Cattle Dog, walks almost entirely on the tips of his toes, tending toward the unguligrade. Ding's trot is an airy gait, much like the trot of a spirited Arabian horse, while Amelia, whose trotting days are nearly over (except when she hears the telltale sound of dog biscuits being lifted from a bowl) plods along a lot like a bear.

Amelia          Ding

Over the next twenty or so million years, the early dog-like creatures gave rise to other lines of carnivores, most notably bears. These were larger and bulkier than canids, and some grew extremely large, like the cave bears of Eurasia (which were vegetarians) and like what is probably the most terrifying predator ever to roam the earth: the great short-faced bear (*Arctodus simus*), who stood as high as a moose at the shoulder and was probably fast enough, at least in spurts, to run down a horse.

Canids also branched out into other dog-like lines in this long period, for example big, almost bear-sized bone crushers something like gigantic hyenas. One of these, known to science as *Epicyon haydensis*, was the size of a bear, and the largest canid ever known. But all the canid-type evolutionary experiments ended in failure—extinction—but for one lineage represented by a canid called *Eucyon*. By about ten million years ago, *Eucyon*'s line ranged around the American southwest, and served as ancestor of all of the dog-like groups of animals living in the world today.

Before long—another two million years, say—at least one species of these canids, something like a small coyote, made its way across the vast land bridge called Beringia from North

America into Asia. In Asia, the environment was undergoing major changes as the rhythmic waxing and waning of the great glaciers produced rapidly changing local ecosystems to which animal and plant life had to adapt. This produced a great variety of canid adaptations. Thus Asia became the original place of emergence of numerous modern canids of various shapes and niches—notably the wolves, jackals, hunting dogs, and foxes. By six million years ago, a wolf-like animal roamed western Europe, and later, various canids spread to Africa. Meanwhile, a number of canids had reached South America, and the smallish, direct ancestor of today's coyote stayed behind in North America—a creature called *Canis lepophagus* (meaning it preyed mostly on hares and rabbits).

By one million years ago, various wolf types had come and gone in Eurasia, one of them giving rise to today's gray wolf (*Canis lupus*). This highly successful creature spread rapidly all over Europe and northern Asia, producing numerous regional versions or subspecies, and eventually crossing the Bering land bridge back into North America some 700,000 years ago. There, it met up with the modern version of the coyote, (*Canis latrans*) as well as another American canid, the dire wolf (*Canis dirus*), a bigger, brawnier animal. About six feet long, it had a large head and huge teeth, but with shorter legs than the gray wolf and it survived in much the manner of a large hyena until a mere 8,000 years ago. (The dire wolf may not have been all that bright, comparatively, given the huge numbers of them who tried to eat mammoths and other creatures stuck in the La Brea Tar Pits that are now part of the Los Angeles Museum of Natural History, and promptly sank into the tar themselves.) By 8,000 years ago, most of the big and comparatively clumsy prey animals like huge bison and giant sloths were extinct, and fleeter prey species like smaller bison, deer, and pronghorns were on hand. In this situation, the greater speed and more coordinated hunting of the gray wolf trumped the brawn and big teeth of the dire wolf, which followed its slower, heavier prey into oblivion. For a long time after its arrival in the Western Hemisphere, the gray wolf was the most widespread canid in the world, living throughout the northern half of the planet.

During the eons since *Cynodictis*, the canids retained their ancient body plan, variations on the theme of the long-distance runner. But the dog template remained what scientists call generalized, unspecialized; it permitted many evolutionary versions. All the other carnivores from weasels to bears and raccoons to cats became fairly specialized. For example, all the cats are strict carnivores. Their cheek teeth contain only carnassials, not flat molars for grinding up plant matter (as do those of most canids). Most cats operate by stealth and short chases. Even lions, which do chase after their prey more than other cats, could never mount a mile or so long chase, which for a wolf is nothing. No one would confuse any cat—from a house cat to a tiger—with being something nonfeline. Cats are cats, period. And bears are bears, period. The closely related giant panda is the only bear alive today who isn't omnivorous: it eats only green bamboo shoots. But the canids themselves proliferated into many more ecosystems, food preferences, and sizes and shapes—to the point where some of them could fool a layman into thinking they were not dogs at all. Canids were *plastic.* They churned out a remarkable variety of creatures.

Today there are thirty-four species (or thirty-five, if that fox on Bali turns out to be a new species) of wild canids, filling niches ranging from the seashore to mountains, deserts, plains, and anything in between, eating anything from insects to fish and clams to certain plants to huge hoofed animals like moose and wildebeest. They come in a vast array of sizes, from the three-pound fennec to the one hundred and fifty-pound timber wolf. One canid species climbs trees, another dives for its food in water. Even so, all of these wild species retain some essential doggishness, as do even the most bizarre creations of the modern breeders of domestic dogs.

Some four hundred deliberately designed variations on the canid theme comprise the breeds of *Canis familiaris*, from a diminutive "accessory" dog carried in a purse on Fifth Avenue in New York to a gigantic Great Dane sweeping clean the coffee table with a wag of her tail, from the shoved-in, pop-eyed face of the Pekingese to the ice-pick snout of the collie. Indeed, the only vertebrate animals who can give the canids, including the domestic ones, a run for their money when it comes to sheer, exuberant plasticity are birds, which range from the tiniest and most accomplished fliers—the exquisitely delicate hummingbirds—to the huge, flightless ostrich. What is the advantage canids derive from all their variety? In a word, they can live successfully in more kinds of environment.

## Doggish Extremes

Most of the wild dogs are not likely to be mistaken for anything else—jackals, wolves, and foxes all are obviously doglike. But the lengths to which evolution has carried canid variety in the wild is perhaps best seen in a creature called *Nyctereutes procyoninodes*. I first came across this animal while leafing casually through the pages of an old book, *The Wild Canids*, edited by Michael W. Fox. There, on page fourteen, was a photograph of a raccoon which I passed by, then did a page-flipping double take. What was a raccoon doing in a book about dogs?

The animal *is*, it turns out, a dog called the raccoon dog, the ponderous binomial hybrid of Latin and Greek meaning "night-roaming, raccoon-like." It has short black legs, a brownish coat, short ears, and what looks like a black mask

*Raccoon dog*

over its eyes. In fact, the "mask" is two large black marks on the sides of its head that also surround the eyes but do not quite meet in the middle. The tail is bushy like a raccoon's but not striped. In all, it looks a lot more like a raccoon than the raccoon's nearest relative, the coatimundi of South America.

The raccoon dog is about the farthest away from the basic dog model as a canid can get, although there are two in South America who have pushed the canid envelope a good bit. The maned wolf looks for all the world like a slightly loony red fox on stilts, and the bush dog looks like an overweight weasel.

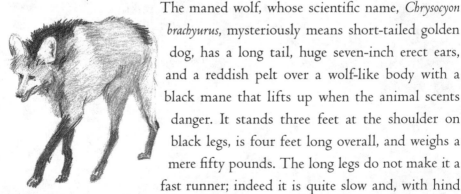

*Maned wolf*

The maned wolf, whose scientific name, *Chrysocyon brachyurus*, mysteriously means short-tailed golden dog, has a long tail, huge seven-inch erect ears, and a reddish pelt over a wolf-like body with a black mane that lifts up when the animal scents danger. It stands three feet at the shoulder on black legs, is four feet long overall, and weighs a mere fifty pounds. The long legs do not make it a fast runner; indeed it is quite slow and, with hind legs longer than the front legs, a bit clumsy going downhill.

The long legs, instead, permit the maned wolf to see over the tall grasses that are common on the savannahs, scrub forests, and marshlands where it lives from southern Brazil to Argentina and Peru. It hunts nocturnally, pouncing on its prey (mostly insects and rodents—and the occasional chicken) like a coyote does, but almost half its diet consists of plants. It is monogamous, a pair coming together to mate and raise the young, but otherwise leading separate lives at other times. The maned wolf is not closely related to any other canid, being the only species in its genus, and from what predecessors it evolved remains a mystery. One might think of it as the only lone wolf but for the fact that it clearly did not derive from wolves, but more likely from some kind of fox.

If you wanted an animal who was the exact opposite of the maned wolf, you would look for something highly social, quite small—maybe five to eight pounds—with foreshortened legs, a slightly thick body, a broad face and tiny round ears. Add to that webbed feet and a short tail, and you have a bush dog (*Speothos venaticus*, meaning true cave hunter, another misnomer).

*Bush dog*

Bush dogs do not habituate caves, though the first bush dog fossils were found in caves. Instead, these dogs live in used armadillo dens or hollow trees in forests and wet savannahs from Panama to Paraguay. They tend to be tawny in front, changing to dark brown or black to the rear.

Bush dogs live in packs of eight or ten, the most social of all the smaller canids, and hunt together during the day; this rounds out most of the ways they are the reverse of the maned wolf. The packs may consist of extended families. They are extremely efficient hunters, preferring to bring down large rodents—even capybaras, who are up to seven times their size—or the flightless rheas who are five times bigger.

These three wild dogs demonstrate how plastic the canid pattern is, and only dog breeders have exceeded this astonishing variety. But aside from the oddballs, the world of wild canids is made up mostly of foxes, in all twenty-three different species on every continent but Australia and Antarctica, adapted to life in woods, swamps, deserts, plains, tropical rain forest, Arctic snow, and ice. In addition, there are three species of jackals which are not unlike foxes, just a bit bigger and with longer legs. Jackals are mostly African, but one species lives north of the Mediterranean. A diminishing number of African hunting dogs still roam Africa, and a little-known dog, the Dhole, is native to India and not greatly admired. The United States—originally only west of the Mississippi but now continent-wide—is home to the superadaptable, canny trickster, the coyote. All of these wild canids are described in some detail in the appendixes at the back of this book, each one something of a marvel in its own right. However, we need to get on with things here—a trajectory that will lead us to the main topic of this book, *Canis familiaris*. To get there we need first to look at the domestic dog's sole progenitor (so far as anyone now knows)—that is, the wolf. There is no way to understand the dog without knowing about wolves.

TEACUP

*Chapter Two*

# Wolves

I met a wolf in Chicago once. She was young and big, and her handler led her into the room on a thick leather leash. The room was part of a laboratory set up where captive wolves were being studied at the University of Chicago in league with the Brookfield Zoo. A pot of chicken scraps and bones was boiling on a hot plate and there was a drain in the middle of the cement floor. I have forgotten the wolf's name; such is sometimes the case, alas, with loves long past. Ignoring the chicken, she padded around the room in circles, staring at me. The handler asked if I would mind if she took away the leash and I said no, I wouldn't mind at all (and this was partly true). A few minutes later, the wolf had put her front paws on my shoulders and stared right into my eyes, her muzzle about a half a foot from mine. She was gorgeous and I found myself profoundly in love.

This is a very different attitude from most people's for

*Canis lupus*

the last ten or so thousand years. When people learned to farm and domesticate animals like sheep, goats, and cattle, they turned against wolves with whom they (as hunters and gatherers in earlier times) had surely coexisted, however uneasily. Wolves became robbers of personal property—that is, domestic animals—and were promptly demonized. They came to be perceived in Europe at least as agents of Satan—foul, dangerous, evil killers. Throughout the Dark Ages, parents terrorized their children—and themselves—with tales of werewolves lurking in the forest attacking the hapless and innocent. Indeed, the dark forests were the place most feared except for Hell, since all manner of supernatural creatures of determined malevolence lived there, not to mention demented humans with mayhem in their hearts. Europeans brought this attitude to the east coast of America and forests were cleared as promptly as possible. Wilderness was bad. Almost 400 years since, many Americans have done a one-eighty regarding forests and other wildernesses as something nearly sacred, to be preserved.

Nonetheless, many Americans, and especially the preponderance of agricultural folk in the West, still hold the view that wolves, along with coyotes, are dangerous, even lethal to humans as well as livestock and should all be eliminated. Wolves were long the subject of a special kind of hatred and, until a century ago, were vigorously exterminated from most of the United States except Alaska—by gun, poison, and trap, with a barbaric vengeance.

In the early 1900s, the federal government took over from citizens the job of exterminating wolves on public lands; for the rangers and others so employed, it was just another job, not a vendetta. Indeed, government rangers began to look more closely at wolves than merely through their gun sights.

And this led to government biologists with the U.S. Fish and Wildlife Service and other agencies doing much the same. Sixty years later, when I met the wolf in Chicago, two generations of wildlife biologists had begun to turn American attitudes about wolves as creatures deserving universal hatred to creatures with whom one could, in a sense, fall in love. And now slowly, gradually, often painfully, wolves are returning to some of their old haunts in the United States and elsewhere.

For eons throughout the Northern Hemisphere, the gray wolf (Canis lupus) was the most numerous of all the large carnivores. Today, its populations are greatly reduced throughout all of its former range, and extinct in much of it, notably England, Japan, most of the lower forty-eight of the United States, and, for all practical purposes, Europe. In all, around the globe there are some thirty-five subspecies, ranging in size from the twenty-five-pound Arabian wolf to the hundred-seventy-five-pound Arctic wolf, and ranging in color from nearly white to black. The gray wolf, in fact, comes in so many sizes, shapes, and colors that it is thought to be the planet's single most diverse species after humans.

Today, Canada has an estimated 60,000 wolves, followed by Russia with some 30,000, a population that has been growing since World War II. In the United States, Alaska has a stable population of about 7,000, and there is a growing population of some 3,000 in the northern lower forty-eight, especially Minnesota and the northern mountain states. It is growing because some Canadian wolves have been sneaking in and because of deliberate efforts to reintroduce wolves into various western locations, in particular Yellowstone National Park. The United States also is home to the last remaining red wolves, Canis rufus, a small group that has been reintroduced into North Carolina after having been rendered extinct in its former range which stretched from Florida across the South to Texas. Smaller than most gray wolves, the red wolf is considered a separate, smaller species, though some earlier observers have suggested that it is a coyote–gray wolf cross. In any event, it has crossbred with coyotes in the last century and so the relict population now reintroduced into the wild from captivity is anybody's taxonomic guess. In late 2005, what one observer thought was a red wolf was seen in Washington, D.C.'s Rock Creek Park, but it was more than likely a coydog, a coyote-dog cross.

The gray wolf is one of the apex predators, or top dogs as it were, of North America. Others are cougars, grizzly bears, and in Mexico, jaguars. Sometimes called charismatic megafauna, and also among the most social of carnivores, wolves are among the most studied, best understood of all carnivores. With their deep, narrow chests and long, thin legs, wolves are made for running, in spurts up to forty miles per hour, and they can cover up to seventy miles a day in their quest for prey. They are opportunistic feeders, eating moose, deer, caribou, elk, bighorn sheep, beavers, musk ox, rabbits, waterfowl, mountain goats—anything they find, along with fruits and other vegetation. If they can be thought of as specializing, it is as hunters of prey larger than themselves, and they have evolved to accomplish this in highly social and highly structured packs led by an alpha pair. Wolves who kill mostly deer typically live in packs of five to seven, elk hunters in packs of eight to twelve. Those who go after the much larger moose and bison will do best with fifteen or more. There is also a social component to pack size: at some point there can be too many for social comfort and the pack splits.

One of the foremost wolf biologists in the world, Minnesotan David Mech, was the first scientist to actually witness wolf kills (from a plane flying over Isle Royale National Park where several packs prey on the resident moose). Research by Mech and others over the years has shown that wolves are in fact not the savage hunting beasts that so many had branded them in their fantasies, given to slaughtering more than they needed to eat and committing other unspeakable felonies. Indeed, a wolf pack out on a foray is successful, according to estimates, only about one time in twenty.

Mech divides the standard hunting behavior of wolf packs into five stages. First is to locate prey, which they do by sight, smell, and probably via a mental map of their territory which can range from fifty to five-thousand square miles. Second, they stalk the prey in a low crouch, all the while gathering signals from the prey about its intent and its strength or weakness. For example, the wolves can probably scent from considerable distance if one of the prey animals is wounded or ill. Third is the encounter, when the prey becomes aware of the wolves. At this point, the prey may run or stand its ground. A large and healthy hoofed animal like an elk or moose that stands its ground can do a great deal of damage to wolves and is not likely to be attacked: wolves have to be masters of risk management. The old, the young, the lame, the ill—these are the ones the wolves look for. If the prey—singly or as a herd—runs (phase four), then the wolves will rush in at high speed, sometimes making a kill quickly. Or the prey may avoid this sudden surge and keep running, followed patiently and relentlessly (phase five) by the pack, sometimes for many miles until the quarry tires. Many hunts are simply called off when the quarry (which, of course, has evolved alongside wolves for eons and participates actively in these affairs) indicates that it has decided to stand its ground.

Such judgments as whom and when to attack are made by

the alpha male and female, and often it is the female who leads the rush, being typically faster (because smaller) than the male. This alpha pair is the very heart of wolf existence—almost always monogamous, and demonstrably affectionate. It is usually only this pair who mate and have young; the rest of the pack—typically all relatives of various generations—help by bringing food to the pregnant female and then to her and her pups, or babysitting while the mother hunts. Raising the pups is a pack responsibility. The pups almost immediately start struggling to see which one is dominant—often in the form of play, but wolf play can be quite rough.

The alpha adults are usually the stronger ones, and those who make the best decisions in the hunt. This ranking can change over the years, the alpha pair eventually being replaced by younger, stronger wolves. Even in such epic struggles, the matter of who is dominant is usually settled by postures and vocalizations rather than outright fights. The dominant wolf will approach another with tail raised, ears erect, the hair on the back raised, and stare right at the subordinate. (I now realize that my Chicago she-wolf was simply putting me in my place.) In turn, a subordinate wolf expresses submission by holding its tail low and wagging it slightly, and flattening its ears back against its head, all the while avoiding eye contact. Such ritualized behavior tends to avoid a lot of dangerous fighting and debilitating physical harm.

A great deal of our understanding of these various signals arises from study of captive wolves, typically unrelated groups of wolves who have to learn to get along with what amounts (at first) to strangers. In the typical days of a wild wolf pack, the group consists of two alphas—a male and female—and several offspring. The dominance of the alpha pair typically goes unquestioned, and whatever pecking order needs establishing among the offspring is accomplished quite easily. As David Mech has shown, in the wild, a wolf pack is not a continuous interpersonal challenge match but instead a well-organized family enterprise.

Indeed, wolves communicate a wide variety of moods and intentions by a complex range of body language, gesture, and even facial expressions, as well as by vocalizations of various kinds. Wolves' most distinctive communication is howling. The eerie howling of wolves is considered the quintessential music of the wild, anciently perceived as ominous if not downright terrifying, but now understood to be a particularly beautiful chorale by which wolves stay in touch with themselves and warn other packs to stay away, and also as a kind of pep rally to rev up the pack for the hunt. Howling would seem to be something like a group expression of community, even affection, and probably a lot of fun for these highly social, family-oriented animals. We will return to all this in later chapters when looking in on how domestic dogs communicate.

(a) self-confidence in social situation    (b) normal attitude    (c) also normal

(d) defensive    (e) actively submissive    (f) fully submissive

Howling has been heard in Yellowstone National Park for more than ten years now as a result of one of the most ambitious programs of wolf reintroduction. Other such efforts have been made in central Idaho and the Black Mountains of Arizona, but none is given as much likelihood of success as the Yellowstone effort for one important reason: Yellowstone is wonderful wolf habitat. As long ago as 1944, the revered land ethicist and government naturalist Aldo Leopold suggested that wolves be reintroduced to Yellowstone, but it wasn't until the 1980s that the U.S. Fish and Wildlife Service began the complicated political task of doing such a thing. They encountered a good deal of resistance (and still do), the locals seeing wolves, if not as Satanic agents, then as significant pests and also symbols of the Western rancher's and outdoorsman's contempt for the land management policies of the federal government.

Yet in 1995, wolves walked free again in Yellowstone, completing its previous roster of wildlife, and the park is now considered the largest intact temperate ecosystem in the world. The addition of wolves did not simply put the area's apex predator back in the picture. The wolves profoundly effected the region, particularly the northern part of the park, creating what scientists call a trophic cascade. One way to think about this meaty phrase is through the words of essayist E. B. White who wrote, "There's no limit to how complicated things can get on account of one thing leading to another." To begin with, once wolves began to prowl the streams and rivers, the elk herds began to spend less time there, moving instead to higher ground where visibility was greater. Over the years, elk had eaten practically every willow and cottonwood sapling; once they started to spend more time elsewhere, the willows and the cottonwoods had a chance to grow again. The same is said for the grasses of the park.

With the willows growing, beavers have moved back (some deliberately reintroduced). In 1996, there was one beaver colony in the northern range of the park; seven years later, there were nine. Beaver ponds in turn are what wolf project leader Doug Smith calls "rich, vibrant oases for insects, fish, amphibians, reptiles, small mammals, birds, even moose." Wolves do tend to eat most of what they kill, but they leave some behind, and twelve different species scavenge wolf kills—including ravens, magpies, bald and golden eagles, not to mention a host of beetles and flies. Grizzlies also benefit—chasing wolves off their kills and gorging themselves.

Meanwhile, the coyote population has declined by about half—the park had one of the densest coyote populations in the West. The two species do not get along, to the coyotes' detriment. This, the biologists report, is going to make life easier for two species the coyotes prey on heavily  pronghorn antelope calves and red foxes. It turns out that one of the places where it is safest to be a pronghorn calf is in the vicinity of a wolf den. That is because coyotes don't go near wolf dens, and wolves don't bother themselves with pronghorn calves.

The elk population has also dropped from some 17,000 to about 9,000 and hunters were quick to blame the wolves, especially since the decline began around the time the wolves were introduced. But wildlife specialists pointed out that a number of factors—and mainly drought which began at the same time—were responsible, not the wolves, who could never kill and eat that number of elk in ten years. Most of those elk preyed on by wolves are the old and ailing or the very young, neither of which have a high life expectancy.

In addition to turning Yellowstone back into what it was before it became the world's first national park, the wolves are adding great dollops of detailed information about wolf biology. Tagged with radio collars and Global Positioning Satellite instruments, their movements can be tracked in exquisite detail, and their hunts more clearly understood as part of a two-way relationship of predator and prey. Their social lives can be studied in greater depth and the rigors of their world more clearly seen. Being the apex carnivore is no picnic. Hunting, as noted, is rarely successful and it can be dangerous. Even the very sociability of the wolf pack—so widely admired now to the point of being romanticized in some quarters—has its downside, called xenophobia. When the youthful members of the pack, often the lowest in rank, have to leave the pack for one reason or another, they have to find another pack to join or found a new one. In any event, they have to travel near or through the territories of other packs, and their presence is rarely welcome. Indeed, scientists at Yellowstone have found that this was one of the major sources of wolf mortality until 2005, when an epidemic killed more than a hundred wolves.

In any event, they are here again, among us. The original call of the wild is back, heard in a few places in the West and Midwest. And with any luck, in the few refuges we can afford them, they will thrive.

*Part Two*

# TRANSFOR-
# MATIONS

*We don't know exactly when dogs were
domesticated but we now have a pretty good
idea of who did it and how it happened.
We consider the importance of pariah
dogs and trash dumps, track some wild
dogs, and look into what dog shows
have wrought.*

TEACUP

Chapter Three

# The Dog Who Came In from the Wild

Just what do people mean when they say this or that animal is domesticated?

Tame, right? It won't freak out if you go up to it and touch its nose. It won't eat you. It likes to be around people. Like cows? They are pretty placid: they'll stand there and stare at you. But anyone who has been kicked or chased by an angry bull (as I was once a long time ago) knows that some domesticated animals are not what anyone would call *tame.* At the same time, you could tame a wild wolf if you put your mind to it and started real early in its life, but its offspring would start out just as wild as the parent was when it was born, and you would have to begin the whole laborious taming process over again. So a tamed animal is not necessarily domesticated.

To truly domesticate a plant or an animal you have to engineer it, turning a wild strain into something different, something a bit more—or preferably a lot more—easily handled as you make whatever use of it that you have in mind. Over enough generations, you might engineer a strain that is so different from its original wild ancestor that your strain simply could not live without you taking care of it. For example, about five or so thousand years ago people in Mexico began to harvest the little seeds of various wild grasses including one called teosinte. They would bring these seeds back to their camp or their little village and some would drop out of their hands onto the ground that was all stirred up from people walking around on it. So teosinte would grow near their dwellings, and the people would favor those teosinte plants that had the biggest, richest, most easily harvested seeds. They would start sowing these bigger seeds nearby in a fairly casual fashion (sometimes called horticulture), thus beginning the long, slow process inaccurately known as the agricultural revolution (revolutions are typically pretty short). Before they were through, the seeds of teosinte were too fat and firmly attached to fall off or blow off the stem.

Teosinte became corn, and it can in no way survive unless people take the seeds of the cob and deliberately plant them. That is true domestication, and in that sense, dogs (and house cats) are not completely domesticated, though the miniature dog breeds would not have a prayer if they were turned out into the wild, what with coyotes and hawks and all. The domesticated dog, *Canis familiaris*, has returned to the wild successfully a few times. For example, the Australian Dingo was brought to that island continent some 5,000 years ago by people in boats, and many of its progeny have lived wild ever since. So dogs are less domesticated than corn, but when they are born they are at least predisposed to live with people. And they have also undergone a large number of changes in anatomy and psychology from their original wolf ancestors.

But even though no dog breed would be mistaken for a wolf if seen clearly and close up, dogs are, in terms of genetics, wolves. Genetically, dogs ranging from Chihuahuas to mastiffs are more like wolves—only two hundredths of a percent difference—than coyotes are, with five hundredths of a percent difference from wolves. This seems counterintuitive and a lot of genetics is just that, not to mention being extremely complicated. But remember, in spite of all the different species names in the genus *Canis*—*lupus, latrans, familiaris* and so forth—they can all interbreed, meaning that they are in practice the same species.

When it comes to the genetic code, DNA, the tiniest variations can lead to vastly different results. And *when* individual genes are expressed, and for how long during the time between conception and adulthood, can also bring about vast differences. Take the skulls of dogs and wolves. The newborn puppies of wolves and coyotes and dogs all look very much alike, and their skulls at birth are very much the same in proportion to their bodies. But the adult wolf skull is larger in proportion to the body than any and all dogs. It continues to grow for a longer time—eight months—than dog skulls, which stop growing at about four months. Except in breeds like Afghans and collies, where breeders have worked hard to make the snout especially long, wolf snouts are proportionately longer than those of dogs, and the teeth are larger. The ratio of brain size to body size is greater in wolves than dogs, and brain size is often taken as an indicator of intelligence.

A number of other important biological changes took place when some wolves gave rise to domesticated dogs, a process that, it has long been presumed, took place over a considerable number of generations. A general reduction in overall size would have come about fairly early, perhaps because of a change in diet (that is, scraps), meaning a bit of malnutrition. In such a situation, natural selection would favor a smaller animal, one capable of surviving better on smaller amounts of food. Also, people probably found smaller animals easier to manage, thus adding their own influence to the process, called artificial selection. Other physical changes included more forward-looking and rounder eyes, floppy ears rather than those that stick up like radar screens, and tails that curve upward over the back. Dogs' coats seem to have changed along the way as well, becoming uniformly tawny in some cases, and piebald or spotted in others. Coat color has been shown to be associated with temperament in a number of domestic animals, and it is possible that protodogs with single-colored or piebald coats were more docile. In other words, genes controlling a lot of what appear to be more or less unrelated features were working in tandem.

A German scientist, Helmut Hemmer, has suggested that many of these physical changes had the effect of changing the animal's alertness or sensitivity to its environment—what he referred to as "a decline in environmental appreciation." Wolves and other wild animals need to be exceptionally alert and react quickly to stress. A domestic animal needs to be docile (at least relatively), lack fear, and have a higher tolerance for stressful events. In this regard, I have always wondered how a dog with its excellent hearing can put up with the high-decibel racket of a city street or a rock band. In any event, less appreciation of the environment would be brought about by a smaller brain, floppy ears (reducing the sense of hearing), and less acute vision.

A tightly curved tail makes communication between dogs less complete than between wolves. Part of the complex body language of wolves is the position of the tail. A wolf that is making a threat or expressing its dominance will hold its tail up above the plane of the back, maybe even vertical, quivering slightly. The opposite extreme is signaled by holding the tail between the legs, or curved past the hind leg. Utter abject submission is shown not so much by the tail but by lying down on one's back and peeing on oneself. Intermediate positions can indicate a possible threat, no social pressure, a depressed mood, and a state between threat and defense. A dog who carries its tail curved tightly over its back is not as able to produce the full subtlety of such signals, thus reducing to some degree its ability to communicate with others.

Many of these traits in domestic dogs are regarded as juvenile holdovers, and retaining juvenile characteristics is called neoteny, the process of remaining like a neonate or baby. Wolf puppies are born with floppy ears and tails that curve upward, but they change to erect ears and tails normally held downward. Wolf puppies do a good deal of barking, but adult wolves bark only rarely and then usually as an alarm call. Dogs inflict a good deal of barkage on the neighborhood throughout their lives for various reasons, and sometimes, it seems, for no reason at all except to make noise.

Of course, many of the more superficial changes brought about in the domestication process—such as the floppy ears and curved tails—can be bred back by means of artificial selection, as in the German shepherd, for example. However, once dogs of different breeds hybridize, creating mutts, they tend to return to the early, domesticated template of floppy ears and curved tails.

Plenty of traits common to dogs and different from wolves are not juvenile holdovers. For example, a wolf does not achieve sexual maturity until it is about two years old; dogs can mate when they are six months old. Wolves—both males and females—can mate only once a year. These differences are clearly the result of variations in hormonal flows. A female dog typically comes into heat twice a year, and a male dog is Mr. Eveready. Our Navajo dog, Curry, fell in love or whatever with our daughter's dog one summer. Curry had been neutered for nine years but the female hadn't. On two occasions I looked out to see Curry and his flame lying there rear end to rear end, looking preoccupied if not actually embarrassed. Nothing could come of it, of course, but I was quite proud of the old boy and I am sure the Navajos would be proud, too.

Obviously, the flow of hormones and neurotransmitters differs considerably between wolves and dogs, which, of course, has profound physical and psychological effects that result from subtle alterations in the timing and length of individual gene expression. Genetically, dogs are wolves, but in most other ways—mentally, physically, behaviorally—they are something else altogether. This should come as no surprise. Dogs evolved to inhabit a completely different niche in the world. The questions are: when did this transformation come about, where did it come about, and how did it come about? To examine these questions, we will have to consult the geneticists, look to the archeologists and paleontologists, be scolded for being silly by a biologist, and study the findings of a renegade Russian geneticist who was exiled to a fur farm in Siberia.

First, the archaeologists. These are the students of artifacts, and like crime scene investigators, they don't believe something has happened unless there is some fairly conclusive proof of it based on real objects—physical remains—that have been left behind and can be precisely dated. Archaeologists are interested primarily in stuff left behind by humans—spear points, sewing needles, dwellings, settlements. They are typically interested in animal and plant remains only insofar as they shed light on such topics as what people ate and what the climate was like. Paleontologists, on the other hand, are interested in the remains of wild creatures, typically in the form of fossils, or pollen. They are interested in, say, the lineage of the Canidae over the millions of years but not so much the domestic dog, since they would consider a domestic dog something of a human artifact and leave it to the archaeologists. However, no one has ever mounted an archaeological expedition the main purpose of which was to locate the remains of domestic dogs. Still, they do turn up every now and then, and more frequently the closer you get to today.

The oldest known fragment of a domestic dog is a mandible (jaw bone) found in 1979 in a grave at Oberkassel in Germany and dated to 14,000 years before the present. But wolf remains have been found in association with *Homo erectus*, a precursor of modern humans, dating back as early as 400,000 years ago in England, and 300,000 years ago in northern China. The association of the two social hunters— humans and wolves—was probably both competitive and relatively intimate. It is not at all unreasonable to imagine that humans from time to time carried around small wolf pups and either ate them or tamed them. Once the tamed ones matured, however, the adults would probably become very difficult to handle and would be killed or shooed away. It is very difficult to tame a wolf: you have to begin at just the right time in the puppy's development (an interval of a few weeks), and it takes a great deal of daily effort thereafter. Even so, one can imagine moments something like that dreamt by poet Brooke Pacy:

> In what cave or on what plain
> did wolf or coyote stretch, yawn, gaze
> from shallow yellow slits into human
> countenance and trust, patiently allow
> a tiny hand to brush its muzzle?

If sometime earlier than 14,000 years ago, some early family or extended family, following game, hunting, and gathering, had managed to tame a wolf puppy—or, better yet, two puppies—they would have had to hold on to them for two years before they reached sexual maturity and had more wolf puppies (who, of course, do not come out tamed). This does not sound very promising, especially for people who were on the go a good part of the year, and probably didn't live much beyond their mid-forties.

On the other hand, one of the most dramatic archaeological finds of domestic dogs was from a site called Ein Mallaha in the upper Jordan valley in present-day Israel. The site has been dated to 12,000 years ago and its inhabitants are called Natufians. These were hunting and gathering people who were on the verge of becoming agriculturalists. They lived in stone houses, used mortars and pestles for grinding wild seeds, and buried their dead in tombs. In one tomb, archaeologists found the skeleton of an elderly human lying on its side, legs flexed, with its hand resting on the chest of a four- or five-month-old domestic dog puppy. In such a place—a permanent or semipermanent settlement—dogs would have benefited from the accumulation of garbage.

Subsequent finds have included a man from this period, buried with two adult dogs in a cave of Hayonim in Israel, and one half of a mandible and complete but compacted sets of teeth found at Palegawra in Iraq, dated to 12,000 years ago. The process of domestication reduces the size of the wolf jaw and, only later, the size of the teeth. For some intermediate period between wolf and true dog, such compacted teeth suggest a transitional form. So maybe it was, after all, a dog, or a protodog, or (as other scholars have argued) just a wolf.

In any event, if we had to rely solely on the archaeological record, we would have to assume that dogs became domesticated before (but not too much before) 14,000 years ago in the southwestern region of Asia that we today refer to as the Middle East, the region where the earliest domestication of livestock and plants also took place along with the origins of monotheist religion and what we call civilization. We could claim, accurately, that the dog was the first living thing to be domesticated. The next animal domesticated was the sheep (about 11,000 years ago in southwest Asia), and the earliest plants were barley in southwest Asia and rice in South and East Asia, about the same time as the sheep. It has been speculated by some that it was the domestication of the dog that gave humans the idea that they could also domesticate other living forms, and this remains the rankest speculation. In fact, as dogs had become domesticated four or so thousand years earlier than sheep, they would simply be an everyday part of the landscape, the process of domestication long since forgotten by 11,000 years ago . . . unless, that is, domestication of dogs was an ongoing process.

Which, evidently, it was not.

According to the geneticists, dogs were domesticated from three female wolves in eastern Asia, and probably China. The precision with which geneticists pinpoint this sort of thing is stunning, and it often puts archaeologists on the defensive. Even more upsetting is when geneticists make estimates of when something like dog domestication took place and the estimate is wildly different (earlier) from what the archaeological record suggests. For example, one of the major players in dog genetics and evolution is Robert Wayne, a molecular biologist at the University of California at Los Angeles. In the early 1990s, he analyzed genetic material from a hundred and forty dogs representing sixty-seven breeds, and from one hundred and sixty wolves from all around the world, plus coyotes and jackals. This study proved not only that dogs descended exclusively from the gray wolf, but suggested that the first dog might "date back 60,000 years, or perhaps more than 100,000 years."

Wayne used what is called mitochondrial DNA, or mtDNA, which is genetic material that exists inside tiny capsule-like organs called mitochondria found within each body cell. These tiny organs provide the energy by which the cells carry on their work. It is quite different DNA from that which inhabits the nucleus of a cell and is mixed with one's mate's during reproduction. Instead, mtDNA is passed on whole and largely unchanged exclusively from the mother to her offspring. The only way it changes through time is by random mutations, and such mutations happen very rarely. When Wayne made his analysis, he found that more mutations had occurred between wolves and dogs than seemed possible in such a short period of time as 15,000 years. Soon people were talking about dogs having arisen as long ago as 135,000 years ago, and this brought about some fascinating speculation.

About 135,000 years ago or thereabouts in Africa there arose what we now think of as *Homo sapiens*, anatomically modern humans. By about 100,000 years ago, they began to migrate out of Africa into southwest Asia and Europe. An Australian anthropologist, Paul Tacon of the Australian Museum in Sydney, soon made the astounding point that dogs, then, could have played an important role in "domesticating" humans or, to be more scientifically correct, turning them into *behaviorally* modern humans. For example, dogs tend to mark their territories by urinating here and there (as every dog owner knows). This might well have taught humans to mark their own territories by inventing art and other symbolic means for marking land. And, of course, it is the invention of symbols that marks the difference between truly modern humans and their predecessors. Also, Tacon went on, the use of dogs to assist in big-game hunting would have given these new figures an immediate edge over the likes of Neanderthals and other primitive humans in Asia, and led to their disappearance.

It turns out that establishing the rate at which the molecular clock of mtDNA ticks is more a statistical art than it is physics and, for a variety of technical reasons, most geneticists who looked into the matter, including Wayne himself, began to shorten the period from when dog domestication took place until today.

In 2002, two articles on dog genetics appeared in the November 22 issue of *Science* magazine that settled some questions for the time being at least. In one article, Peter Savolainen of Sweden's Royal Institute of Technology reported on examining the mtDNA of 654 dogs around the world. He had begun studying dog genetics to enable police to tell what breed of dog left hairs at a given crime scene, and he had spent many years snatching hairs from dogs at dog shows and writing away to dog people around the world for samples. It is an axiom of genetics that where you find the greatest genetic diversity of a given creature is almost certainly the place the creature originated. The site of the greatest genetic diversity among humans is Africa, which conveniently matches the fossil record, so few scientists are unhappy about the finding. Similarly, Savolainen found the greatest genetic diversity among the dogs of East Asia, and suggested China as the likely spot. (There is a nice irony to this in that during the Cultural Revolution, Mao Tse-tung banned dogs from China as being bourgeois.) Savolainen also found that almost all dogs (95 percent) could be traced back to just three females. This means, of course, that a few yet-to-be-identified, rarer lineages of dogs could have come from elsewhere, leaving room for more genetic studies.

Yet another matter was settled in that same issue of *Science*. Jennifer Leonard of the Smithsonian Institution and her colleagues on the study including Robert Wayne worked with dog remains from thirty-seven archaeological sites in Peru, Bolivia, and Mexico—remains that were dated as far back as 1,400 years ago, and all of which were pre-Columbian. They also studied eleven remains from the Alaskan permafrost. With this material they produced a family tree of wolves, modern New World dogs, and ancient New World dogs. It showed that the ancient New World dogs had derived from Old World wolves. It also indicated that the lineages of ancient New World dogs have all died out, quickly replaced by dogs brought here by Europeans. In other words, some humans who came across the Bering land bridge or paddled along the warm Japanese current to Alaska and points south and peopled the hemisphere brought dogs with them. A lot of dioramas in museums and paintings showing these early Americans will have to be updated with the addition of dogs.

Yet just when the dogs accompanied people to the New World is not clear. The date of the first human entry is controversial among archaeologists but signs of human habitation have been found in western Pennsylvania that unarguably date as early as 16,000 years ago. This would put dog domestication back well before 15,000 years ago . . . but only if these earliest pioneers indeed brought dogs. So far there is no way of telling if they did. There is no reason to think that there were no other incursions of people after the first one, however, and dogs could have come with later ones. The oldest known remains of a dog found in North America so far are some 9,000 years old.

So where dogs arose is fairly certain. And that it happened only a few times seems fairly certain. When and how this amazing transformation took place thousands of years ago is harder to pin down. One way to find out how it came about would be to do it over again—to domesticate some gray wolves—but such an arduous effort is not necessary, thanks to the Russian geneticist, Dmitry K. Belyaev, who was exiled to Siberia after World War II for not paying homage to the state's non-Darwinian genetic theories.

By the late 1950s, however, the USSR had joined the rest of the world (in genetics, anyway), and Belyaev began an experiment in animal domestication, importing silver foxes—a subspecies of the red fox, *Vulpes vulpes*—from a fur farm in Estonia. The goal originally was to produce foxes who were a bit easier to handle. With thirty males and a hundred vixens, he wound up mounting an elaborate, multigenerational breeding program, ultimately involving more than 45,000 foxes. He selected foxes for breeding with only one trait in mind—tameness. When foxes reached sexual maturity at eight months, they were tested for tameness and sorted into three classes. Foxes that ran away from handlers were put in Class III. Class II foxes allowed themselves to be handled but showed no particular emotional attachment to humans. Class I foxes were friendly to handlers, wagging their tails and whining. After six generations, the experimenters had to create a new class—IE—for the "domesticated elite." These foxes avidly sought out human contact, whimpering, sniffing, and licking handlers before they were a month old.

With each generation, a greater percentage of pups were in Class IE.

Physical changes began early on. By the eighth to tenth generation, the coat color changed, mainly as a result of a loss of pigment, making white patches. Then came floppy ears and curled tails. After some fifteen to twenty generations, foxes were turning up with shorter tails and legs. And after forty years and as many generations, the tame foxes had a longer reproductive season (though not more than one season per year as with other domesticates). Their skulls were smaller in height and width, and their snouts shorter and wider. They also had lower levels of activity in the adrenal glands—which respond to stress—and higher levels of serotonin, which tends to lower aggressive impulses. The handlers who took puppies home to raise found them good-tempered, as devoted as dogs, and as independent as house cats but capable of forming deep bonds with humans. They were not domesticated dogs, but they surely showed themselves to be on the way to something analogous to *Canis familiaris.*

One of Belyaev's silver foxes, domesticated

Of special interest in Belyaev's foxes is that the physical and mental changes that took place in the course of domestication were impelled not by choosing foxes based on size, color, obedience, or any other characteristics, but on a single behavioral characteristic: tameness. And another stunning discovery is that the foxes traveled this considerable distance to becoming a vulpine version of the domestic dog in less than a human life span. Even so, it is hard to imagine that a small band of seminomadic hunters and gatherers could have accomplished the domestication of some wolves into dogs by simply taking advantage of a couple of tame wolves who were not so scared of humans that they would hang around camp and feed on scraps and bones thrown into the dark. In the first place, the Belyaev experiment was extremely sophisticated and deliberate, while our little Late-Pleistocene family could have had nothing like a domesticated dog as their goal. It would have all had to be more or less accidental. But even more to the point, it took the Russians some 45,000 foxes over forty years to come up with a bunch of foxes that act like pet dogs. In other words, Belyaev and his experimenters had a huge universe of foxes from which to select and breed. People wandering around China fifty or a hundred thousand years ago would probably not have run across even a hundredth of that number of wolves in a lifetime.

So how did the transformation of wolf into dog come about? Many now say that the wolves took the lead and domesticated themselves. One of the leaders in the wolves-did-it school is Raymond Coppinger, an outspoken biologist at the University of Massachusetts at Amherst. Coppinger loves trash heaps and dumps. He found the very well-managed dump serving Tijuana, across the border from San Diego, to be one of the most beautiful places he had seen. That, of course, is because it supported an interesting array of feral dogs. Except for what he called the "leather collar" faction that visited daily but lived and slept in houses in the neighborhood, the dump's dogs lived there year round. Most of them had distinct flight distances when it came to the human scavengers in the dump, some of whom live there year round as well, and some of whom are specialists who arrive early in the morning to collect rags or other things to sell. Flight distance is how close a dog (in this case) will let a human get before it flees, and also how far it flees before stopping. In a few cases, a dump dog would live with a human, sharing a cardboard carton house, but most of the dogs lived alone or slept in small groups, and went about their scavenging solo, paying little attention to the humans with whom, in many cases, they competed—and vice versa. It sounds like a remarkably courteous place, if not exactly a peaceable kingdom.

Inspired by such places here and there around the world, Coppinger came up with a reasonably plausible—if not slam-dunk—scenario for the transformation of wolves to dogs. The Coppinger hypothesis accords with the current findings of the archaeologists that dog domestication probably took place somewhere around 15,000 years ago, and that is because there had to be fairly good-sized aggregations of people in permanent settlements, or at least seasonally permanent settlements, for the process he postulates to take place. (Coppinger goes after mtDNA estimates of anything much earlier than that with all the diplomacy of a Viking pillager.)

In various parts of the world, people began settling down into permanent or at least semipermanent villages at least 4,000 years before they began to farm. And aggregations of people create large aggregations of low-grade waste including bones, bits of meat, rotten plant matter, even human excrement. Such aggregations in turn attract all manner of scavengers—insects, birds, rodents and other small mammals, even a few wolves whose flight distances were lower than the average, who could put up with the proximity of humans. Here then was a brand new niche that some wolves—the "tamer" ones—found they could adapt to.

At this point, natural selection would take over. Wolves who could do well enough to thrive at such dumps would begin to differ slightly from those wolves whose flight distances would not permit them to be that close to human settlements. As the dump-loving wolves reproduced with each other, their tameness would probably become more and more pronounced. And before long, an advantage at such places would be conferred upon those wolves who were smaller overall and had proportionately smaller skulls and therefore smaller brains.

What possible advantage could there be, you ask, in having a smaller brain? The brain is a ferociously expensive organ. Its growth and maintenance takes a huge fraction of the total energy available to an animal. To follow the complex pack-hunting life of the gray wolf requires a great deal of brainpower; to scavenge in a dump on low-grade food that doesn't try to escape requires less brainpower. Not only that, but a large brainy wolf with a numerically greater flight distance is going to be at more of a disadvantage in a dump than a smaller, less brainy "wolf" with a smaller flight distance. When old Grog stumbles out to the dump for a midnight pee, the smaller creature will stay longer and run less far than the larger one which, once surprised, runs away sooner and farther and stays away longer, thus getting less food. Such incremental changes add up—and as we saw with Belyaev's foxes, they can add up fairly quickly. Wolves could have turned into village dogs in relatively short order.

So permanent settlements are needed to create the niche that transformed a handful of wolves into dogs. And according to the geneticists, the settlements had to be in eastern Asia, most likely in China.

Or would a semipermanent settlement be sufficient? After all, if people spent, say, half the year amid a rich population of huntable animals and collectible plant food, and then migrated to another such a spot when winter was on the way, whatever these dump scavengers were—protodogs?—could follow along. Indeed, they would probably have been welcomed, being at the very least a portable larder in a pinch. And people in fairly large groups were doing just this sort of thing— at least in western Asia and eastern Europe some 25,000 years ago or more. About 24,000 years ago, at a site called Donyi Vestonice in what is now the Czech Republic, a considerable group of people lived, if not year round, then most of the year in shelters of stone and hides, hunted in the river valleys, collected wild plants, stored food for the winters, made ceramic figurines, produced woven clothes, and created ample middens of waste. Wolves surely took note of such places and possibly began approaching them. In any event, we still don't know exactly when some wolves, who had changed hardly at all in millions of years, were transformed into dogs, the most protean, shape-shifting mammals on earth. The matter now seems to rest in the hands of archaeologists in China.

But a question remains: why did the quality called tameness have such a profound effect, changing a wolf into an animal with a smaller head and a curved tail and all that? What caused some of the genes of wolves to express themselves differently, at different times?

The answer may well lie in an organ that dwells in the front of the throat and, in humans, looks something like a butterfly: the thyroid gland.

The thyroid gland emits the thyroid hormone, which is chemically the same in all animals with backbones, and which performs an array of important functions. That it is the key to domestication and perhaps even to the evolution of new species out of old is argued in *The Rhythms of Life*, a 2006 book by Susan Crockford of the University of Victoria in British Columbia. Among the numerous functions of the thyroid gland, it "controls both brain and body growth from just after conception to adulthood . . . all aspects of reproduction, and all the steps involved in basic metabolism. . . ."

In addition to mediating the growth and color of hair, it "synchronizes the body's response to stress of all kinds . . . In other words, thyroid hormone is responsible for coordinating all of the other hormonal responses necessary for an individual to adapt to conditions of the environment that change on a daily and seasonal basis."

The thyroid emits its hormone in a rhythm that is specific to a given species (but may vary slightly among individuals of a species). It is variations in the rhythm that appear to affect the timing of gene expression as an animal develops and matures. Wolves who had a higher tolerance for the stress of being around people would presumably have different rhythms of thyroid hormone, which in turn would promote other physical and psychological changes in those realms under the coordination of the thyroid—which is practically everything that occurs in the animal domestication process, be they goats, cows, silver foxes, sheep or, of course, dogs.

That's right. Except for when exactly it happened, and where exactly, the mystery of dog domestication has evidently been solved.

Young Curry

*Chapter Four*

# Pariahs

hat would the first dogs have been like? If Ray Coppinger is right, they were village dogs, what many people think of as curs— junkyard dogs that give noble Rex a bad name and have since time immemorial. Craven scavengers slinking around in filth and waste, disease-ridden low-lifes scratching at fleas and mange. In fact, such dogs are to be found practically everywhere there are human settlements and one semiofficial name for them is pariah. *Pariah* is a Hindi word meaning essentially the untouchable caste. (As noted earlier, scavengers get a bad rap among humans, which is at least biologically hypocritical: it is fairly evident that through most of the eons that we were in the long and slow process of becoming *Homo sapiens*, we got a lot more of our red meat from raiding carcasses killed by carnivorous animals than from animals killed by us.) In any event, pariah dogs have given rise, it seems, to a number of feral dogs including (some say) the Dingo of Australia, the New Guinea Singing Dog, the Carolina Dog, the Canaan Dog of Israel and a host of others including the barkless Basenji that originated in Africa. And, of course, the actual Pariah Dog of India.

The Pariah Dogs of India are not what we would call a breed: they come in various sizes and colors—most are brown and white but some are black, especially in those areas where leopards prowl at night. Like wolves, they tend to live and scavenge in packs. Unlike wolves, they do a lot of barking. Highly territorial, they defend their turf regularly from canine interlopers, but are docile in the presence of humans, like most beggars. Once thought to have been the direct ancestors of the Dingo, they have been transported by humans throughout much of the Old World and Africa, possibly having given rise to the Rhodesian Ridgeback.

All these pariah dogs of today inhabit a foggy realm that lies between wild and domesticated, between the physiology—and psychology—of wolf and dog. Some of them conceivably could be direct descendants of the first village dogs, unchanged for more than fifteen or so thousand years, never *owned*. If so, they are what biologists would call commensals, similar to Norway rats (also called vermin), or house sparrows that most American bird lovers wish had never been brought here from England, the vermin of the bird feeder. On the other hand, most of the pariah dogs living today were at some point domesticated and then became feral, severing their connection to humans except to hang around, tolerant of human propinquity as long as they were in turn at least tolerated.

Most commonly the Dingo is ginger-colored, varying from

*Pariah dog*

more reddish to more yellowish, but they come in virtually all colors. Males can stand two feet at the shoulder, and weigh up to fifty pounds. It retains a number of wolf-like traits—a tail not curved upward, once-a-year mating, and also hunting in packs made up of an alpha pair and their kin. Like wolves, they rarely bark. They have been tamed: Konrad Lorenz, the great pioneer of ethological studies, had one and reported that it "harbored the warmest feelings . . . but submission and obedience play no part in these feelings."

Evidently the Aborigines made little or no effort to domesticate (redomesticate) Dingoes. They play with them, fondle them, but do not feed them. The Dingoes had to make a living on their own, often by swiping the Aborigines' food. Also, they would have to be driven away when the men were hunting, since Aboriginal hunting depended on stealth. Why then would the Aborigines tolerate their presence? In 1969, the anthropologist Richard Gould visited a group in Western Australia. Most of the people he visited had never seen a European. In and around camp were some nineteen Dingoes, cringing, skulking, robbing food. But at night, the Aborigines and the Dingoes snuggled up together for warmth in the near-freezing desert nights. This is what you might call symbiosis, where both parties gain something from the association. The German-born philosopher Raimond Gaita of London grew up in Australia and reports that a truly cold night would be considered a three- or four-Dingo night.

Once Europeans and their livestock arrived in Australia, the Dingoes became the enemy. While their normal food was kangaroos and smaller marsupials, they took happily to sheep and the Australians took action to eradicate them, much as American ranchers set out to clear their world of wolves and

*Dingo puppy*

coyotes. Eradication proving not quite possible, the Australians built the longest fence in the world to try to segregate the Dingoes from livestock (as well as the remaining population of hairy wombats). It stretches more than 3,000 miles from the Great Australian Bight to the east coast of Queensland, cutting off the southeastern third of the continent. The fence's effectiveness is arguable—large amounts of poison are sometimes added—but a more subtle eradication scheme was already in place. Dingoes breed freely with domesticated dogs, and about 70 percent of all Dingoes today are hybrids to some degree. Reverse efforts to eradication have now been undertaken to maintain the purity of the remaining "pure" Dingoes and they have been named *the* Australian national breed.

Dingoes are not considered particularly vocal animals; they communicate via moans, howls (single and group), and what are called bark-howls. The howling would seem to be much like that of wolves—to bring members of a pack together or to call in a mate. When especially alarmed, a Dingo will emit several barks followed by a howl as a warning. The moan seems to be restricted to warning other Dingoes at a water hole that you are coming in for a drink.

As late as 1975, a chapter in *The Wild Canids* was titled "The Origin of the Dingo: An Enigma." That it was a modern equivalent of the primitive, early or (better) "basic" dog was fairly clear, though no one could assert for a certainty that the Dingo had ever been domesticated. The preponderance of thought was that it never had been. No one was certain when it arrived in Australia, though it had to have come by boat since Australia was never connected to mainland Asia and no canid, never mind a mating pair, was going to swim across some fifty miles of seawater. By the same token, the Dingo could not have arrived much before 12,000 years ago, because it has never been found on nearby Tasmania, which separated from Australia at that time as sea level rose with the melting of the great glaciers of the north.

Modern genetic studies (by Peter Savolainen, who placed the first domestication of dogs in Southeast Asia and probably China) have now shown that the Dingo probably arrived in Australia some 5,000 years ago. This is about the time that Chinese people were beginning to colonize the archipelagos between Asia and Australia. And, it seems, the Dingo arose from three domesticated dogs in Southeast Asia, not the pariah dogs of India as some had suspected because of skeletal similarities.

Another version of the Dingo has lived in the steep highlands of New Guinea for some 5,000 years—the New Guinea Singing Dog. Called Singers by their fans, they are in essence living fossils, having arrived in New Guinea some 5,000 years ago as domesticated dogs, and having been isolated from all other canids until the 1950s. Many say that the Singer is the most primitive domesticated dog anyone knows of.

Singers are about half the size of an Australian Dingo, reddish-orange or black with tan tips, and unknown outside of tribal New Guinea until 1957, when the first pair was taken from Papua to a zoo in Sydney by a Sir Edward Halstrom. It was seen as a very odd dog indeed and was pronounced a new species, *Canis halstromi*. A number of features of the Singer are unique among canids. Their eyes are as reflective as a cat's eyes, presumably an adaptation to hunting at night. They have cat-like flexibility, good for jumping and climbing in the steep gorges of the highlands. They have several vocalizations distinct from domestic dogs and wolves, most noticeably the especially melodious communal howling they are named for.

Their vocal equipment includes a long palate that hangs down in their throat like a human uvula—a feature unknown in other canids. Like the wild canids, Singers have but one heat per year.

So far, only five other Singers have been brought out of New Guinea (these were taken to a German zoo) and all of the Singers outside of New Guinea (about 300) are descendants of these seven animals plus one from the Sydney population. A New Guinea Singing Dog Conservation Society sprang up in the 1990s, with a view to preserving the wild population and keeping better track of the genealogies and breeding of the captive population. They use the word captive because they believe the Singer to be a wild dog, never domesticated, and thus a unique species.

Yet another potential cousin of the Dingo turned up in the 1970s in, of all places, the Savannah River nuclear site, a 300-acre reservation of woods, marshes, and decommissioned nuclear equipment in South Carolina. In fact people had seen these ginger-colored dogs lurking around for years—the typical Southern "yaller dowg" as far as anyone knew. But I. Lehr Brisbin Jr., a University of Georgia ecologist, began to think that these evident "strays" looked a lot like the Dingoes he had begun to study along with the process of dog domestication.

The Carolina Dogs were what some call red-brown, others golden, and others ginger. They had the characteristic sharp fox-like nose and prick ears, with a tail curled over their backs. Brisbin began collecting them—from pounds and from the wild. He wondered if they might be directly descended from the dogs that accompanied some Asians across the Bering land bridge into North America. He compared the Carolina Dogs to a Korean breed, the Chindo-kae, a free-ranging dog on Chindo Island that has been free from hybridization with other breeds. It is a dead ringer for the Carolina Dog.

The Carolina Dog breeds not two times a year like *Canis familiaris* and not once a year like wolves. Instead, it breeds three times a year. Uniquely among canids, they dig odd little pits that exactly fit their snouts. The pits are dug chiefly by females and only in the fall. What purpose they serve is anyone's guess. Brisbin wonders if they aren't obtaining minerals from eating the soil. They hunt in packs, running down even venomous snakes which they kill by snapping them in the air. Preliminary genetic studies (of mtDNA) suggested that the Carolina Dogs are near "the base of the domestic dog family tree," meaning that they are probably primitive dogs or, as some have it, the basic dog. Further genetic studies could either confirm this—making the Carolina Dog something very much akin to the original dogs brought to the New World—or they could show that the Carolina Dog is more recent and, left to its own devices and the forces of natural selection, bred its way back to something resembling the original, basic dog.

Many of the free-ranging members of the breed remain shy and standoffish when it comes to humans, though a number of them have become devoted companions. They are not standoffish when it comes to other dogs, however, so they are being severely hybridized in the wild. Meantime they are championed by the Carolina Dog Association, which sponsors research on them and seeks formal recognition of these dogs as a distinct breed.

The Canaan Dog is a distinct breed of domesticated dog that arose only recently from some relatively undifferentiated pariah dogs. In 1934, Professor Rudolphina Menzel had fled from Austria to what is now Israel, an area known as Canaan and also as Palestine. An expert trainer of service dogs, she was later asked by the Jewish Defense Forces to train some dogs for military service. None of the usual breeds for such work could thrive in the extreme aridity and heat of Canaan, and Menzel soon noticed that the local pariah dogs were used by some of the Bedouins as guard dogs. They required little food or water or other creature comforts—they were desert dogs. Selecting some pariahs that most resembled collies, she created her foundation stock, and during World War II and Israel's war of independence, the dogs served well in the military. Later, others were trained as seeing-eye dogs. The Canaan Dog is now recognized as a standard breed in Israel and part of the Herding Group of the American Kennel Club. It is one of the rare dog breeds that does not seem to suffer congenital disorders such as hip dysplasia or retinal deterioration, perhaps because it is too recently a breed to have accumulated these genes.

Such an exalted state as recognition of breed status does not await those pariah dogs I am most familiar with, the Rez dogs of the American Southwest, specifically those of the Hopi and Navajo reservations which are both in northeastern Arizona, though Navajo lands extend into New Mexico and Utah as well. These are modern breeds and mutts who have been abandoned or born on the reservation and have had to fend for themselves, living the feral life. It is a fairly rapidly changing population. One can see the turnover in major sires: one year most of the pups in an area look a lot like Chow chows; two years later, most of them seem to have a lot of Blue heeler showing. You do not see a lot of elderly dogs on the reservation.

These dogs are almost never treated with the spiritual reverence that American Indians are famous for according to game animals. Instead, they are ignored (at best) or actively brutalized and shot at randomly (at worst). Indian kids will play with a litter of new puppies, carry them around by one leg often as not, use them as toys to be thrown, and often just kill them. Hopi adults would not be caught dead letting a Rez dog in the house: they are considered dirty and worse. My wife and I know only one Hopi family who actively like any of the ever-changing group of scruffy dogs that hang out in the neighborhood. The man of the family would be happy to bring a favorite or two in the house if his wife (Hopi women own the houses) would let him. Whenever my wife and I visited this house over the years, as many as three or four dogs would cautiously greet us, ears back and head low, tail wagging tentatively. Our friend's house was probably known to them as a place where the occasional handout was available. On the other hand, the peaceable atmosphere among the dogs around that house was puzzling to me. One would think they might be more competitive, even territorial, having found a sucker. And that is precisely what a scientific study of Navajo Rez dogs showed.

In the 1980s, one of the great researchers of dog behavior, Marc Bekoff (now at the University of Colorado), made an extensive study of some Navajo Rez dogs with the help of a group of students. He studied those dogs who hang around small clusters of rural homes separated by great distances from other such clusters (something like our Hopi friend's neighborhood), and also dogs who were more free-ranging, centered around dump sites away from human dwellings.

The dogs in the human communities were mostly loners who would center their territory on one or two houses where they could get the occasional handout, and they guarded these places jealously from other dogs. The more free-ranging ones, whose existence centered around the outlying dump, were more likely to go about their lives in what appeared to be loose packs. Puppies were born in dens and the mothers would be gone for considerable periods finding food for them. As a result, the littermates formed stronger bonds with each other than with the mother, and packs often consisted of a few unrelated adults and a younger pair of littermates that split off from their parental pack.

Not all Navajo dogs are pariahs. Since the arrival of the Spanish in the American Southwest in the sixteenth century, the Navajos have traditionally been pastoralists, their economy and culture dependent upon sheep. And over the centuries, the Navajos developed various (not at all pure) lineages of sheep dogs. Once a sheep dog puppy is identified, it is considered largely sacred. Children are not allowed to play with it, and it is sequestered away from human contact, living, sleeping, and eating in the sheep pen. Later, a Navajo family will be able to send the sheep off into the surround to graze, herded and protected only by the sheep dog.

One time several years ago, Susanne and I were driving along a dirt road near Nazlini, a small Navajo settlement south of Canyon de Chelly. In the desert scrub ahead we saw a herd of sheep begin to set out across the dirt road, the bell of the bellwether sheep ringing cheerfully. We slowed to a stop, at which point a tiny little mutt, hardly out of puppyhood, left the sheep and approached the car, barking furiously. It threatened us and our automobile with mayhem if we were to come any closer, and we marveled at how bravely it shouldered its responsibilities.

In life, Damon Runyon wrote, the odds are six to five against. Except for the Navajo sheep dogs, for Rez dogs the odds are woeful indeed. Only about a third of any litter of pups survives as long as four months—the time at which they become totally weaned and independent. They fall prey to diseases such as distemper, to predation by coyotes, eagles, and the like, to starvation, and, of course, to humans. Once they are independent, the mortality continues, with territorial challenges from other dogs being added to the list. The free-ranging existence, Bekoff wrote in what may be taken as an understatement, "may reduce survival markedly." Indeed, it appears from this study and others made in such places as Baltimore and Newark as well as Tijuana, that such dog populations would dwindle over time to zero were it not for the fairly predictable addition of abandoned dogs and puppies that replenishes them.

Over the years, Susanne and I and some of our daughters have adopted a number of other Rez dogs in addition to Curry the Navajo and Teacup the Hopi-Cochiti mix. One daughter brought from Hopiland home to Washington, D.C., a little brown and white puppy with a pink nose, who our Hopi friend named Pookhoya, pronounced *Poka hoya* and meaning dog-little. The dog, a female, wound up called simply Hoya and lived to the age of fifteen. During this period the daughter gave birth to three children, and when Hoya, a bit grumpy in old age, snapped at them, the mother explained to them that Hoya had become part of the household before they had, so they should treat her with respect. Hoya went on to have puppies from some unknown but presumably black sire and Susanne's sister took one of them, the others being spread around the neighborhood. For all we know Hoya's legacy continues to this day in the nation's capital.

\* \* \*

As hard as it may be to imagine, it is highly likely that man's best friend arose from dogs who lived the pariah's unpromising existence. It is probably not too far out to imagine that what made this possible was how attentive such pariah dogs got to be to the humans in their world—how observant. They had to be observant lest they get kicked or miss a chance to take a morsel from the two-legged creatures in their midst. They had to identify the humans' moods, their body language, their facial expressions. Indeed, they would have begun the process of identifying themselves with humans.

This is borne out by a series of experiments run by anthropologist Brian Hare of Harvard and three colleagues. They set out to test how well domestic dogs and chimpanzees could carry out what the experimenters called "an object choice task." An experimenter hides a piece of food in one of two boxes, brings in the animal to be tested, and then gazes at, points at, and touches the box with the food in it. Chimpanzees (who, of course, are genetically our closest animal relative) found the hidden food at the same rate as chance would dictate. Dogs, however, performed well above chance. So Hare and his colleagues opined that since many canids, especially wolves, are highly social, this might be a capacity—reading human cues—that was common to several kinds of canids. Or it might be that dogs typically have much more experience with humans than chimpanzees do. Or, finally, it might be that in the process of domestication, natural and artificial selection both have pushed dogs to develop special skills in the realm of social cognition and communication.

To see which if any of these hypotheses were true, they brought in some wolves and tested them against dogs. Again the dogs chose correctly well above chance, but the wolves performed at the level of chance. So much for the canid-wide explanation. What then of the idea that dogs learned to do so well because of their association with human owners? They brought in a bunch of puppies of various ages, some raised in human families, and some raised only with littermates and mothers, but not humans. All the puppies performed as well as the adult dogs right from the beginning. This was not something they learned. It was an inherent skill. Hare and colleagues wrote that "as a result of the process of domestication, some aspects of the social-cognitive abilities of dogs have converged . . . with those of humans."

So the dog's ability to read human signals, like pointing and looking in a given direction, are in the same category as the curved tail and the floppy ears—things that came about simply because of domestication. Just to be sure, Hare and colleagues went on to run the same experiments on Belyaev's foxes. The tamed foxes reacted just as skillfully as puppies and adult dogs, and did so spontaneously.

Q, as they say, ED.

JUNO DISCIPLINES JUPITER

## Chapter Five

# Dogs of Old

Some ten or so millennia after dogs were domesticated, they were a common feature of the landscape and fulfilled many roles chosen for them by humans. The ruling classes of ancient Egypt, for example, kept kennels of coursing or sight hounds—something like today's greyhounds—to put on hunts of ibexes and rabbits for the amusement of guests. Egyptians imported small pointy-eared dogs and what look like early versions of the Basenji from farther south in Africa, and later large mastiff-like dogs from Anatolia and the Middle East—war dogs that the Egyptian military incorporated into their armies.

A dog god became an important figure in the Egyptian pantheon. This was Anubis, always depicted black, with the head of a dog or a jackal. Anubis was associated with death, and served as guide for the dead to a meeting with Osiris, where they would be either consigned to death forever or resurrected. Thus Anubis, the dog god, was also god of resurrection. It appears that toward the end of the hegemony of Egypt, hundreds of thousands of dogs were mummified and used as offerings to Anubis; these were small dogs, probably puppies, who were raised, killed, and mummified for sale to Anubis pilgrims—probably the first puppy mills in the history of the world.

Outside of Athens, where all dogs were banned (probably out of fear of rabies), the great cities and towns of the Greco-Roman era in the Mediterranean were, like Egyptian towns and cities, overrun with pariah dogs. But the Greeks and Romans also had various hunting dogs (both sight and scent hounds), small companion dogs, and the big mastiff-like dogs called Molossians after a tribe of people who lived in Epirus in Greece. Records show that the ancient Greeks gave at least some dogs names and regarded them with as much affection as dog lovers do today. The Romans used the big Molossians as guard dogs for flocks and temples, draft animals, and fighting dogs in gladiatorial entertainments—attacking lions or humans or each other—and, of course, militarily.

Modern students of these ancient times and dogs refer to the Roman Mollossian guard dogs as *Canes familiaris villatici*. Sheep dogs were assigned the name *Canes familiaris pastorales*, and hunting dogs the name *Canes familiaris venatici*. This all sounds terribly scientific, but, of course, not one of these three essentially made-up dog types was anything like a species or a breed. Tracing today's breeds back to ancestral dogs known only from illustrations and written descriptions is a bit of a mug's game, and over the past couple of centuries, students of pure breeds have driven themselves crazy in the attempt, desperately seeking "agreement" between, say, the skulls of Irish wolfhounds and Scottish deerhounds and tracing them back to a putative ancestor called *Canis palustris* (swamp dog), which others have called the ancestor as well of the likes of Spanish water dogs (that is, spaniels) and Eskimo breeds of the Spitz type like the Keeshond. One has to think that such anatomical agreements or disagreements can mean only little in the mysterious history of this most protean of mammals, *Canis familiaris*.

*Canis palustris* cave art

People keep trying however. Recently a group of Spanish scientists added to *Canis familiaris palustris* four other superprogenitors: *C.f metris-optimae* (German shepherd, collie, and other herding dogs); *C.f. intermedius* (basset hound, beagle, Dalmatian, Golden and Labrador retrievers, pointer); *C.f. leineri* (harriers, such as the Afghan hound), and *C.f. inostranzewi* (Great Dane, Newfoundland, Rottweiler, Saint Bernard). At some point, either the geneticists will work out the whole story or everyone will give it up as an unfathomably bad job, and not worth the effort. In the meantime, many breeders of today's pure-bred dogs are wont to trace their breeds' histories back to Egyptian dogs or other ancient ones. Keeshond fanciers, for example, are convinced that it derived directly from *Canis palustris.*

At present there is rarely any good evidence for such claims. A popular modern guide to dog breeds speaks of the ancient breed, the Canaan Dog—which actually didn't exist until World War II.

For most of their time on the planet, dogs have been busily mixing themselves up to the point that, with a few exceptions like the Dingo and the New Guinea Singing Dog, their lineages are almost totally opaque.

*Canis palustris* cave art

Similarities in appearance from one dog to another can just as easily be the result of what is called convergent evolution: two quite different dogs put to the same task can, given enough time, wind up looking alike.

By 1200 A.D., the Chinese achieved what could almost be called a breed. Various versions of the pug dog existed there, with little flat faces, the nose pushed in with the nostrils almost as high as the forehead, the bodies reduced to about a foot in length. In something like the Chinese fetish for binding royal women's feet to keep them tiny, the miniaturization apparently was achieved by methods we would deplore, such as starving the puppies, keeping them in cages too small for them to grow, and other rough (and useless) measures, along with what had to have been selective breeding for smallness. They were the dogs exclusively of Chinese royalty, closely held little lap dogs, but in 1860 the French and British sent troops to China to fight the second Opium War. Having stormed the imperial palace, they turned the empress's bug-eyed little pugs loose, as well as bringing some back home where they immediately became highly popular.

Practically everywhere dogs have joined up with people, there have been ambivalent feelings and beliefs about them. That great power of most of European history, the Roman Catholic Church, was highly ambivalent. Of course, dogs, like other animals, had no such thing as a soul, and were given to nasty practices like promiscuity and eating offal. At the same time, some dogs were known for a nearly perfect loyalty and for heroic feats protecting their masters, and were given praise therefore. This, of course, could be taken too far. The Church had to undo the beatification of a greyhound that a cult had declared a saint for its role in saving an eleventh-century French knight's baby from a serpent. At the same time, Jesus was often referred to as the Hound of Heaven.

Later, as what we call the Renaissance got underway, the philosopher René Descartes concluded that not only did animals have no souls, they had no emotions, no feelings. They were essentially living machines. In the last two centuries, animal scientists—zoologists, psychologists, and others—have gone back and forth on this very ancient dichotomy (a subject that will be taken up in later chapters).

Regardless of philosophical disputes, many people living in what we refer to as civilized cultures have felt free to abuse animals, by outright fits of cruelty or by placing them in bondage, such as dogs who pulled tradesmen's carts or turned spits and other devices. Not until 1840 did the British found the Royal Society for the Prevention of Cruelty to Animals, and the American version came along twenty-six years later in New York City, from which the movement spread across the nation in fairly short order. An outgrowth of this movement is the Humane Society of the United States, which sponsors animal shelters throughout the country and works for improved animal treatment and animal rights (as do several other organizations). Recently, Wayne Pacell, president of the Humane Society, proposed that dogs be referred to as Canine-Americans in order to advance animal rights. Feline-Americans? Equine-Americans? Reptilian-American has an interesting ring to it.

It is often said that the way a culture or civilization treats its domestic animals is the measure of how truly civilized it is. No civilization we know of is likely to come off with an A+ in this regard, but if we go back a couple of thousand years and cross the Atlantic from Great Britain, we will see just how ambiguous a measure of civilization the treatment of animals can be. For example, the Aztecs, a bloody lot if ever there was one, engaged in nearly continual human sacrifice and, most scholars agree, cannibalism. And they sold dogs by the thousands in their markets for food—usually castrated male dogs.

It was mostly the nobles and other upper class Aztecs who regularly dined on dog, since it was expensive.

The Mayans, whose civilization preceded the Aztecs, also ate dog, and their predecessors the Olmecs probably did too. In their cases, deer and turtles were the most frequent remains in their middens, but dogs were a strong third among the Olmecs, and about fifth in Mayan middens. It should be noted, in defense of what readers of this book would like to think was a widespread taboo, that none of these societies enjoyed the use as food of domestic animals such as sheep, goats, and cattle that were staple parts of the diets of Europe and the Middle East beginning some 10,000 to 11,000 years ago. The only other domesticates available to these great Mexican civilizations were turkeys.

To the south, as early as 3000 B.C. and probably a lot earlier, people living along the western coast of South America were practicing agriculture and developing elaborate societies—civilizations came and went over time. By 500 A.D., for example, people called the Moche had herds of camel-like animals—llamas and alpacas—which they used for wool but also for about 85 percent of their meat. Dogs were next, followed by guinea pigs.

In southern Peru, archaeologists have been excavating the cemeteries of people called the Chiribaya, whose culture ran from about 900 A.D. to 1350 A.D. They have found more than forty mummified dogs buried with blankets and food alongside their human masters. The dogs look something like small Golden retrievers, and it would appear that the Chiribayas believed that they shared an afterlife of some sort with them—a status previously seen only in ancient Egypt. The archaeologists have joined Peru's kennel club in trying to establish if the dogs were an actual breed and if they have any descendants alive today. In any event, with the Moche and Chiribayas we have two quite distinct attitudes to dogs.

Around the time the Chiribayas drifted into oblivion, a small group of people called the Incas suddenly began a grand campaign of expansion and soon enough had control of an empire stretching 2,500 miles, over which they sought to impose their particular values which included the worship of the sun and a strict prohibition against eating dogs. We don't know just how successful they were in imposing their diet on their subjects—one group of whom were the Huanca, whom the Incas called *guana alcomico*, meaning wild camels who eat dogs.

The Incas achieved an amazingly efficient system for controlling their empire even though they did not have the benefit of the wheel or writing, and possessed a rudimentary means of counting. Yet they produced little in the way of what we might call high culture—art, for example. And they did not eat dogs. On the other hand, the dog-eating Mayans developed an elaborate kind of writing and a calendar so accurate that it can be compared to our own, while the artistic flair of the Aztecs is unrivalled by any North American culture with the possible exception of the Indians of the Pacific Northwest. So some old civilizations ate dogs and some didn't. Dogs continue on the menus of several Asian nations.

Among the North American Indian peoples, dogs served many purposes, from supporting actors in creation stories and other mythology (which is a snobby word for other peoples' religions), to beasts of burden, hunting assistants, and, for some groups, food. Before the horse escaped from the Spanish and became the central core of Plains Indian culture, the Indians of the region used dogs for hunting

*"Suncca," a dog evidently bred originally by the Incas*

and hauling. These Plains dogs, according some early accounts by Europeans, were difficult to distinguish from wolves (at least at a distance) and may have mated with wolves from time to time.

Four of these Plains dogs could haul most of a family's belongings on travois, two long poles affixed by harnesses to the dogs and loaded with a pile or packet of goods—or meat obtained in a hunt. The dogs could haul such loads some six miles a day, thus relieving the women of a considerable burden. Women typically owned and trained the bigger puppies in a litter to the travois. Dogs may also have aided men in the hunting of bison, which had been done on foot for millennia. With a herd of horses, far more belongings could be hauled (again by the travois) and the iconic large tepee was born, something the dogs could never have hauled. The dogs' role in hunting diminished now that hunter/warriors could ride right along with the stampeding bison and pick them off with arrows and later rifles.

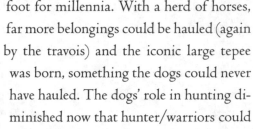

*Rock and Great Basin, c. 200 A.D. Note leash*

A recent book, *Mountain Spirit*, tells of the *tukudika*, a band of Shoshones—people who lived from California to Montana. Tukudika means meat eaters, and they came also to be called the Sheep Eaters. They lived in what is now Yellowstone National Park and, for a great deal of their diet, they hunted bighorn sheep, those hard-to-hunt masters of difficult rocky terrain. Large and resembling wolves, the tukudikas' dogs were trained to try to herd the bighorns, to which they responded by climbing higher. The dogs would follow, and the sheep would keep on climbing until they reached a place where a human hunter, waiting in hiding, killed them.

The status of "Eskimo dogs" in the Arctic was ambiguous.

They helped in such tasks as locating seal holes in the ice and snatching a hapless seal up through the ice, or assisting others with the hunting of such large beasts as musk oxen. At the same time, they would typically be fed once every couple of days at best, and were never fed whale meat since it would be demeaning to the whale to be eaten by so ignoble an animal. A common belief was that dogs were born without souls but acquired one upon being given a name. The so-called Eskimo dog was described as large and wolf-like, with a bushy tail curved over the hip. It had a thick undercoat overlain by long hair. Its teeth were smaller than a wolf's.

Indeed, there seem to have been two main kinds of dogs in North America—large ones and small ones. Otherwise, there was not a great deal of differentiation—except in two known cases, both from the Pacific Northwest coast. This is the region famous for its huge carved totem poles and astoundingly graphic artwork. The Pacific Northwest peoples are remarkable for having a highly stratified society with hereditary no-bility and other elaborate cultural features *without* the benefit of agriculture. So lush and rich was their territory that they could gorge

*Steatite dog effigy pipe from Copena Mound, Alabama, 200-660 A.D.*

on an abundance of fish (chiefly salmon), seals, whales, and other easily gathered sea food, as well as hunting (in a pinch) inland for deer and other game. They built huge plank houses, and participated in elaborate rituals, as well as carv-ing out long war canoes and engaging in a nearly continu-ous stream of skirmishes and wars.

In the northwest region of what is now British Columbia, people referred to as the Hares, the Tahl Tans, or the Tlin-gits maintained what seems to be pretty close to an actual breed of dog, known as the Tahl Tan bear dog. Not a great big creature as the name suggests, it was small, black and white, with erect ears, a bushy tail curled over its back or hip, and hairy feet for traction in the snow. One early observer described it as mild of "countenance, with, at times, an expression of demureness." Demure or not, it was a feisty dog about the size of a fox terrier and it specialized, it seems, in holding bears at bay until its Indian masters could kill them. In 1900, the bear dog lost its job to the .44 caliber rifle, and it was almost extinct in 1942 when the Canadian Kennel Club recognized it as an actual breed. Forty years later it was no longer with us on the planet, but specimens have survived in the form of skins and skeletons in the Royal British Columbia Museum in Victoria.

Nancy Dill, the last Tahl Tan bear dog

The archaeozoologist and student of the thyroid Susan J. Crockford and two colleagues undertook a thorough analysis of both skeletal remains and mtDNA to determine if the remaining specimens showed that this was a purely aboriginal (pre-Columbian) animal or one that had been inbred with the arrival of Europeans and their dogs. The skeletons showed that the Tahl Tan bear dog was not, as some said, too small to be aboriginal, and the mtDNA tests showed that it was certainly an aboriginal breed of dog, at least on the maternal side.

Even more secure as an actual pure breed in pre-Columbian times in North America is the dog found among the Salish peoples who inhabited the coast and islands of southern Vancouver Island and south across Puget Sound to the northern coast of Washington State as well as the Olympic Peninsula. Evidently the Salish had two types of dogs—the medium-sized village dog, something like a coyote in appearance, and a smaller, longer-haired dog that they kept for wool. This sheep surrogate is called the Wool Dog and it is almost surely a pure breed because the people who kept it accomplished what every pure breeder must. It is said that a prerequisite of maintaining a pure breed is some form of writing, to keep track of matings, sires, dams and all that. But the Salish could not write. On the other hand, they would have perceived immediately what happened if they let village dogs breed with the Wool Dogs: the puppies would have shorter hair than their Wool Dog parents. Obviously, the Wool Dogs had to be isolated, to breed only among themselves. You did not need to know how to write to figure that out. The solution? The Salish reported that they kept the Wool Dogs on an island with dried food buried in the ground for the dogs to find during those times that the humans could not be present and watch over them. So the Salish (and presumably the Salish women) maintained a true pure-bred dog for some largely unknown time, possibly centuries, and used their wool for weaving blankets and other textiles.

During the early times of European contact, brightly colored blankets came available, and the Salish weavers stopped making blankets from the Wool Dogs, whose numbers declined and who were allowed to breed with the village dogs. By 1858, according to Crockford, the Wool Dog was considered extinct as a breed.

But by then dog shows were on the brink of becoming widespread, and the world of the Fancy would soon produce hundreds of pure-bred breeds, all conforming to precise— even fanatically precise—specifications.

Curry lying on Jupiter

## Chapter Six

# Good Breeding

In 1859, Charles Darwin published *On the Origin of Species by Natural Selection*. That same year, the world's first oil well was drilled in Titusville, Pennsylvania, and the first formal English dog show was held at Newcastle-upon-Tyne, featuring pointers and setters. The notion was afoot in highly class-conscious England that if one bred dogs to tighter physical standards (that is, appearance), it somehow "improved" dogs. Many marriages among the British aristocracy were arranged, too. Soon it was highly lucrative to have a dog-show winner, just as it is to own a Kentucky Derby winner, and fakery and corruption—of the sort that hang like a miasma over many sports—were not far behind.

By way of stemming this unfortunate tide, in 1873 the British Kennel Club was established, with the American Kennel Club born a year later. They functioned as registries but also, as historian Mary Elizabeth Thurston has pointed out, "as a union of sorts, lobbying on behalf of the breeding industry, and orchestrating a monopolistic series of interlocking shows through which members had to work their way toward championship standing." Pedigree became as important in the dog world as it was in the upper reaches of Victorian society.

Breeders were on the way to being dog designers, and fashions in dogs rose and fell much as they did in clothes. For example, when the British soldiers brought Chinese miniatures back home to England after the Opium War, they were an instant hit, and soon enough were turned into a proper breed with elaborate specifications. This was, of course, the Pekingese, which was standardized to a certain maximum weight (eleven pounds for males, twelve for females) and to a double coat with a profuse mane and a feathered tail. They can come in any color except albino and liver, which are impermissible. The Pekingese, along with other toy dogs with severely shortened muzzles, are also examples of some of the unintended consequences of producing a greatly flattened face. It leads to respiratory problems as well as a reduced sense of smell, and the eyes have so little room in the skull that the slightest blow can cause an eyeball to literally pop out of its socket. It is interesting to note in this regard that even as the formal dog show was becoming something of a craze in England, a baroness, Judith Blunt-Lytton, became a lonely voice protesting the notion that a pedigree meant a superior creature. Though she herself was a toy spaniel fan, she said that the inflated money value of pure breeds encouraged the creation of unhealthy features in dogs including "idiocy" in some spaniels. A tension has existed ever since between those who breed to type and those who consider such efforts a kind of genetic abuse. We will return to this later on in the chapter.

Before the strict standardization of breeds that arose with dog shows, there were, of course, different strains or types of dogs that were, at least roughly speaking, breeds. Historian Mark Derr recounts that George Washington was an active breeder of dogs, and bemoaned the times when a bitch in heat would escape to an unplanned mating. Washington "achieved relative uniformity [in appearance] by drowning puppies that did not match his conception of what his hounds should look like." Most such breeding was done with what are called working dogs—hunters, herders, guard dogs, and the like. There were dogs known as retrievers, but there were not yet dogs known as Labrador, Golden, or Flat-coated retrievers.

The Lewis and Clark expedition that assayed the land between Missouri and the Pacific in the early years of the nineteenth century was accompanied by an early version of the Newfoundland called Seaman. On one occasion during this great overland voyage, an apparently crazed (probably scared) bison crashed into camp and raced around knocking over equipment and breaking gear, coming near to trampling some of the men. Seaman chased the bison away and thus saved the expedition members from harm and possible death. For this and other benisons, Seaman was memorialized by having a northern tributary to the Blackfoot River named Seaman's Creek.

Newfoundlands became all the rage in New York City in the 1850s and, along with a fancy address, conferred high status upon their owners. By this time the populations of eastern and some midwestern cities were growing rapidly and with the influx of people came the influx of dogs—a lot of them mongrels running loose, or mongrels owned by the poor. Many city dwellers saw the dogs—especially the mongrels— as chiefly a public health problem, what with the fear of rabies and the addition of canine waste to the equine waste that fouled the streets. This latter problem remains with us today in many cities and towns where governments struggle to enforce dog regulations of one kind or another.

The notion of breed purity was afoot by the mid-1850s, and by the 1880s the dog show entrenched it in the minds of many as the cardinal quality of dogs. As a result, the general run of mixed breed dogs—aka mutts—would be looked upon with increasing contempt. Never mind, of course, that new breeds were, and still are, produced by mixing various breeds, as in the case of the Doberman, a combination of German pinscher, Rottweiler, and Manchester terrier. In that sense, every pure breed began as a mutt.

But then the founding mutts—the ones combining the traits and appearances the breeder had in mind—must be inbred with their own kind to perpetuate the desired traits. There is nothing particularly wrong with inbreeding—so long as it doesn't go on too long without a bit of outbreeding. This is one of the problems with puppy mills, those breeders who churn out a particular breed of dog for the pet stores to sell. The difficulty of all this breeding to type (in other words, a strict adherence to the approved appearance of the breed) is that it creates unintended consequences. Just as the breeding of silver foxes for a single trait—tameness—led to the physical and mental changes associated with domestication, so breeding for appearance only to maintain the so-called pure blood of the breed has made most breeds subject to a great many genetic afflictions. This does not mean that every individual member of a breed will suffer one or more of these afflictions. It means that the breed is prone to them to a greater degree.

One of the most common of these afflictions is hip dysplasia (HD), in which the ball at the top of the femur is misshapen and grinds away cartilage in the socket. This leads to a host of arthritic problems that can cascade into severe lameness and pain. In one list of health problems in eighty-eight breeds, forty-one are prone to hip dysplasia. Painkillers can help, at least temporarily, but in the worst cases the dog must be put down. Hip surgery is becoming common. Another of the most common genetic conditions is Progressive Retinal Atrophy, which is exactly what it sounds like.

Within some breeds, an affliction can be very widespread. For example, one out of three Dalmatians and one out of six English setters will become deaf in one ear or both. Deafness also afflicts the Australian Cattle Dog (meaning, among other things, that I may have to teach our Cattle Dog Ding sign language). The American Kennel Club's Canine Health Foundation helps finance research into many of these genetic disorders, including the deafness of Dalmatians and Australian Cattle Dogs, in this case a study carried on at Michigan State University. The foundation is involved in studies of a long list of breeds and each is described in the AKC's Web site.

In all, Donald F. Patterson of the University of Pennsylvania's vet school found more than 370 of these genetically produced afflictions or susceptibilities in some two hundred breeds. (A list of some popular breeds and some of their health problems can be found in the appendixes.) Of course, dogs are subject to other diseases of the contagious kind—such as distemper and influenza. For many if not most of these, veterinarians supply diagnosis, vaccines, and antibiotics. But as dogs travel more from country to country, vets have to be on the lookout for exotic diseases as well.

There is something of a silver lining in all this. About half the diseases that afflict dogs also afflict humans. With the spelling out of the dog genome and the human genome, both of which have been done, there is great hope that by comparing them and hunting for disease-causing genes or gene clusters in the dog genome, medical scientists may find genetic cures for congenital problems in humans. As early as 1999, for example, a scientist at the Stanford University School of Medicine located the genetic mutation responsible for narcolepsy in dachshunds, Dobermans, and Labrador retrievers. Researchers then had an idea of where to look in the human genome for a similar mutation. As Mark Derr points out, the Seeing Eye organization "effectively eliminated hip dysplasia from the Labradors and German shepherds it breeds as guide dogs." Dog geneticists are certain how to breed against many congenital afflictions, research that has also received help from the AKC. The task typically involves outbreeding—that is, admitting other similar breeds into your breed's gene pool—and this goes against the grain of those breeders who tenaciously hold on to the notion of "pure bloodedness."

Meanwhile, geneticists are getting close to being able to tell what breed a dog is from a bit of DNA. Recent studies have identified eighty-five breeds with 99 percent accuracy, though in one embarrassing case they mistook a beagle for a huge mastiff-like guard dog. Elaine Ostrander of the Fred Hutchinson Cancer Research Center of the University of Washington points out that even though scientists can assign a breed with some accuracy by viewing genetic material, they cannot tell how it will behave. Indeed, it has become clear that there is likely to be more behavioral diversity within breeds than between them.

Genetically, there seem to be four separate groupings of dogs—three share physical characteristics, or geography, or uses as guards, herders, or hunters. These are recent breeds, developed within the last two centuries in Europe and America. A fourth grouping consists of older breeds that appear to be more closely related to wolves, dogs who are not usually grouped together. They include the Asian Chow chow, the Siberian husky and Alaskan Malamute, the Sharpei, Shih-tzu, the much manipulated Pekingese, the Saluki (a Middle Eastern dog), and the African Basenji. That the diminutive Shih-tzu with its flowing locks is close to the wolf seems to be a kind of genetic alchemy. Another surprise is that the German shepherd is genetically closer to mastiffs and boxers, which is to say guard dogs, than to herding dogs which its name implies.

Will there be new breeds created in the years ahead? Will the Labradoodle, a combo of the Labrador and poodle, survive as a real breed? Or will it be a mere fad? What purposes would new breeds be created to fulfill? Dogs love to hunt, and to run, and fetch, and herd. In any given week in the United States, hundreds of dog events take place—herding trials, obedience trials; agility contests; dog shows involving all breeds, all working dogs, or other categories, or single breeds. And in any park that is large enough to have dogs running freely, chasing balls thrown by their owners or other informal, unorganized activity, one may also see some dogs leaping into the air to catch a Frisbee as it sails by. Of course, some are better than others at this sport. Excellence here calls for speed, terrific agility, and particularly good judgment about the arcing trajectory of the Frisbee—a kind of instinctive understanding of calculus. Breeding dogs to produce championship Frisbee catchers could be next.

The Frisbee dog.

That would certainly liven up the Fancy, now wouldn't it?

# Part Three

# THE DOG'S WORLD

In the past fifty years, more and more
scientific analysis has been brought to bear
on this ancient companion of the human
race, and the glass though which we
see them, their lives and how they
perceive and manage their world is no
longer so dark.

PUPPIES FROM A NEIGHBOR'S DOG

*Chapter Seven*

# Puppies

In much the same way that a caterpillar isn't a moth until a major transformation takes place, a newborn puppy can usefully be thought of as the larval form of a dog. In its first two weeks (or thereabouts) it cannot see, cannot hear, and apparently cannot smell much of anything except the presence of its mother, and that only very close up. It cannot bark or growl, but it can whine and yelp if it crawls away from its mother and littermates, or experiences hunger or pain or cold. It can crawl only very slowly, pulling with its front legs, head wagging slowly side to side, and only forward or in circles, but not backward. If the wagging head bumps into either a littermate or mother, the larva-like puppy moves closer to it. If the puppy strays too far, the mother will get up and fetch it in her mouth.

The puppy can suck but typically it needs the mother to get it all lined up. Then the puppy, again typically, pushes alternately with its front feet against her breast which stimulates lactation (and also rouses the other puppies to get in on the feast). In return the mother licks the rear end and genital area of her puppies, which stimulates them to urinate and defecate, which she then cleans up by licking, thus keeping the nest or den sanitary.

With few exceptions, dog fathers have nothing to do with any of this. Among wolves and most of the other canids, the male participates at least by helping to feed the mother if not helping to feed the pups. Not dogs. Practically all dog puppies grow up in single-parent homes. Why this is so is not clear.

The puppy, then, is deprived at the beginning of its life of the three most important senses with which it will one day confront its world—sight, hearing, and most of what will later develop into a sense of smell thousands of times more acute than ours. All it knows about its new world is what it can touch or taste. Some experimental evidence suggests that the newborn puppy's brain is capable of the most primitive learning—for example, if you were cruelly to get one these little fellows to accept milk from a rubber nipple (not easy) and then put something bitter on it a few times, it would reject the nipple thereafter, regardless of the bottle's contents.

Most of the nerve fibers of these newborns have yet to develop their sheaths of myelin, a fatty substance that promotes the exchange of signals between nerves. The nerves work unsheathed, but fifty to a hundred times more slowly. For some breeds it is common practice to dock the puppy's tail, which is to say, to cut it off. This was done to our little Australian shepherd, Jupiter, and I cannot think of a good reason why it was done. Our Australian shepherd–Cattle Dog mix Juno was allowed to keep her tail and it looks fine to me. Some hunting dogs' tails are docked to keep them from getting fouled up in thickets, one is told. The Doberman suffers both the loss of its tail and the docking of its ears. Frankly I find this all scandalous, like the old Chinese habit of binding the feet of royal women, a kind of mutilation.

Docking is usually done within three days of birth, before (it was once thought) the puppy would feel any pain, We now know that the puppy does feel the pain but simply doesn't react to it right away because the unmyelinized nerves work so slowly. But even so, this regrettable and in most cases pointless practice continues.

The few nerves that already are properly sheathed at birth are little those that go to the mouth and jaw, and the part of the auditory nerve that affects balance. If you turn a newborn puppy on its back it will struggle to get upright. In any event, by the unfinished nature of its sense organs and nervous system, a puppy is insulated from most of the world around it, and this is actually a great benefit. For about a fortnight it is sheltered from most things that might trouble it psychologically in any serious way. In the late 1950s, a scientist, John Paul Scott, and his colleagues called this period in a puppy's life the neonatal period, which means newborn.

Scott and his colleagues built what they thought of as a dog school in Bar Harbor, Maine, a very upscale summer resort town on Mount Desert Island. There, they raised hundreds of dogs from five breeds—shelties, cocker spaniels, wire-haired terriers, Basenjis, and beagles. Over decades they observed these animals in the minutest detail, hoping to elucidate the question: how much (or little) does genetic heritage have to do with an animal's behavior? Their results were published in a landmark 1965 book called *Genetics and the Social Behavior of the Dog*. It remains a foundational volume for anyone professionally involved with dogs as breeders, trainers, or medical and biological scholars. Scott's team found four distinct and important periods in a dog's trajectory to adulthood—the neonatal period, the transitional period, the period of socialization, and the juvenile period.

We will get to all of these, but in the meantime, more recent scholars have suggested that all this is preceded by the prenatal period, when such hormonally inspired states as high emotionality from stress on the part of the mother can cross the placenta and may affect the unborn. Also, in Scott's neonatal period, later scholars have discovered that being handled by humans at this time in their lives makes them better able to handle stressful situations as they grow older.

After some thirteen or fourteen neonatal days comes the transitional period. As Scott and his coauthor John L. Fuller wrote, "the puppy comes into the world not as a simplified version of an adult but as an animal highly adapted to an infantile existence . . ." Indeed the puppies of most canid species look very much the same, differing primarily only in size and color. They are perfectly adapted sucking machines. After two weeks, the puppy "undergoes a transformation in behavior which is almost as spectacular as the metamorphosis of a tadpole into a frog." The transition takes about a week, beginning with the first opening of the eyes and ending with the opening up of the ear ducts. One can only imagine that the arrival of so much sensory information in so short a period has to be, in some doggish way, thrilling.

The retinas of two-week-old puppies, like their vision overall, are not fully formed (that will take another six weeks) but sight begins to take over from touch as a way of orienting themselves to their world. By the end of the week, they will begin to respond visually to foreign puppies or dogs or humans at a distance. They begin to leave the nest or denning site and go elsewhere to defecate and urinate, which they do now without maternal stimulation, though she continues to look after their hygiene. As early as two weeks, some puppies will begin to growl if given a bone, and they soon begin playful fighting, clumsy little wrestling matches. This play starts once the puppy is able to move backward in response to a visual stimulation—what Scott called a visual startle response.

By the end of the transition period, most puppies can and often do wag their tails. Tail-wagging, Scott and Fuller wrote, "appears to have no directly adaptive function, but is simply an expression of pleasurable emotion toward a social object." At about this time as well their first teeth begin to erupt, the upper canines which can be felt just below the gums at about twenty days. And they begin, however harmlessly, to bite and chew.

The transition period is said to be over when the puppy's ears open up and it is startled by sudden loud sounds. And at this point they matriculate into the period of socialization. Having been insulated from much of the world in their first two weeks, by the end of their third week they enter a longish period when they are highly sensitive to the new world they perceive.

By four weeks, they have a sense of the space around them, and their brains are now developed enough that they can control their body temperature and their metabolism. (The newborn pup's brain is developed only enough to control heartbeat, breathing, and balance.) They can now stand up on all fours and walk. They can lap milk from a bowl and deal with soft solid food, which the mother begins to provide via regurgitation, as needed. By five weeks they can stay awake if they desire to. At about five weeks or so, the mother will begin the weaning process, by seven weeks growling and snapping at the pups when they try to feed, and walking away, making the pups follow her to suckle while she stands up. Usually by ten weeks they are all weaned and eating solid or semisolid food provided by the mother or by humans. Experiments (in this case with German shepherds) have shown that if a mother is extremely aggressive while weaning her pups, they will usually grow up to be less sociable with humans, and perform less well on certain tests like fetching a ball. This weaning process, which seems to the sentimental to be dreadfully harsh, is when the puppies learn about who is the boss. The mother's behavior earlier is simply that of the constant caregiver. Now the puppies begin to see that they must, in a sense, compromise.

By seven weeks, the mother will start to leave the nest or den for long periods of time and the puppies begin to move around as a unit, following one another. Play behavior begins in earnest—more lessons in power and compromise. This is a tremendously important time: if a puppy is isolated from others at this age, it will wind up being hyper-aggressive to other dogs. If it were to be put in with a group of cats instead of dogs, it will later on avoid dogs and associate with kittens—in effect, its psychological species altered.

At this time the puppies become strongly attached to their immediate neighborhood as well and show considerable distress if moved from it. This intensifies in the sixth and seventh week, and then begins to ebb. Eight weeks, often considered the time to "rehome" a puppy, is now seen as too early, causing unnecessary distress. The ideal time to remove a puppy from its birth home and take it elsewhere seems to be about twelve weeks.

Meanwhile, right at the beginning of the socialization period, at three weeks, puppies will approach a quiet, still human being, wagging its tail (which most sentient humans take as a personal reward, not unlike the smile of a baby) and nosing the human's shoes. Continuing studies of this period showed that the most sensitive time is from six to eight weeks: this is when social relations with familiar humans and other dogs are most easily developed. Becoming socialized—with other dogs or with humans—is its own reward. Puppies will become attached to humans whether or not they receive a reward like an edible treat. And evidently in this highly sensitive period it only takes a short bit of human contact—minutes, not hours—a few times a week.

On the other hand, working against the pleasurable sensations of socializing, the puppy also grows increasingly fearful of casual strangers, as well as of leaving the neighborhood or being left alone. The period of socialization in which puppies begin to show the first signs of adult behavior appeared to Scott and Fuller to be a "critical" period. They suggested that if, for example, some puppies went without human contact during this time—from about three weeks to twelve weeks— they would never take to humans. Period.

At twelve weeks, Scott and Fuller wrote, the period of socialization ends and the puppy enters its juvenile period. Further research has shown, however, that the socialization period's end is not abrupt, as the neonatal period is, and also that the period of socialization is not the all-or-nothing situation that Scott and Fuller said. It is possible to socialize a dog if it has missed its "critical" period (scientists now prefer to call it a "sensitive" period.) It just takes longer and requires more regular attention.

When my wife and I rescued our Navajo dog, Curry, we followed him to an underground den in a large sheep pen and pulled him out, shivering, in what seemed like a panic. He was, we learned, about twelve weeks old at the time and, if anything, he had learned that human beings were bad news, especially little ones. He probably hated to leave his familiar territory and might well have thought of himself as a sheep. In any event, he was terrified of the car, terrified of our house, terrified of us. He was terrified that doors would slam on him. After about a month, he would let Susanne or me touch him, but only on the stern end of his back and only with one hand. Eventually, he discovered the bed and, once on it, he would let us scratch his head or his back. For eight years, that was about it: he never let anyone else get close, except other dogs in the house.

Then one day our granddaughter Gracie, age three, saw him lying down near Susanne as she worked at her desk. So Gracie lay down across the room and slowly, gradually inched closer to him. Then she reached out and touched him and pulled her hand back. She repeated this for more than a half hour, touching finally on practically every place on his body. Since that afternoon, Curry has been insistent (almost to the point of being a pest) that he get his share of touching, petting, hugging, etc., and from anyone who happens to be around. I have been told that such transformations are rarely so abrupt.

At the beginning of this sensitive period, puppies startle at loud sounds and sudden motion, but they soon learn to ignore sounds and motions that have no significance for them. And as noted they begin roughhousing, really harmless play-fights where they paw and mouth each other. By seven weeks, however, around the time they are being weaned, with the mother growling and snapping at them, puppies of some breeds begin ganging up on one littermate, typically the smallest. And in some breeds struggles for dominance begin, which continue after the puppies' first twelve weeks as the period of socialization drifts into what Scott and Fuller called the juvenile period. Dominance behavior, when one male and one female become the alphas as in wolves, is not found in all dog breeds. For example, in Scott and Fuller's studies, the beagles and cocker spaniels rarely exhibited such behavior. On the other hand, it was pronounced in their terriers. When it occurs, it is usually fairly early in the socialization period and it may arise from competition for food, or for space, or even for the attention of a human. Domestication seems to have had profound effects on the expression of dominance among dogs. It is much less intense than among wolves, if it exists at all. And where it does exists, it seems to begin at about four weeks.

People often ask us which of our six dogs is the alpha. In fact, we see few signs of any kind of pecking order. The oldest female sometimes grumbles at one of the other dogs and, less and less now, stands over them to exert her idea of hegemony; the mid-age Australian shepherd—Cattle Dog will snarl if any dog comes too close to her food bowl, and the youngest of the six, the Cattle Dog, always maneuvers to be the first out the door and otherwise gets his way, though if he gets growled at he rolls over in hopeless submission, then goes about his business.

When puppies enter the juvenile period, all their sense organs are fully developed. What has been very rapid growth slows down at about sixteen weeks, which is also when adult teeth begin to emerge. The puppy now has two-thirds of its ultimate size and about 80 percent of its brain volume. All of its early experiences have caused its neurons to grow larger and make more connections; the richer the puppy's experiences, the more complex its brain.

It will now stray far away from its denning site, investigating its domain. This period is characterized not so much by new behaviors (though males will begin lifting their leg to urinate), but by the maturing of motor skills and the development of strength and stamina. The juvenile period comes to an end at about six months when the puppies attain sexual maturity. Even though they are capable of mating, however, they will continue to grow until they are about two years old.

For now, it is clear that events that take place in a puppy's socialization period have profound effects on its behavior in later life. An early illness that keeps a puppy from its normal interactions with its littermates can lead to any of a host of problems: dominance-type aggression (which includes attacking the owner), fear of strangers, fear of children, separation-related barking, and inappropriate sexual behavior. At the same time, if puppies are kept in kennels for too long (say, twenty-four weeks), they may wind up fearing other dogs, or traffic.

Even the place and circumstances in which a puppy was born and raised has at least a statistical chance of bringing about problems, or not. In the 1990s, Andrew Jagoe surveyed the owners of 737 adult dogs, asking about the owners themselves, health problems the dogs may have had, early experiences, and what kind of "problems" the adult dogs exhibited, as well as where the dogs were obtained. Problem dogs, it turned out by a significant margin, came from pet shops and the streets. Dogs from pet shops were significantly more prone to dominance aggression and social fears. Dominance aggression was also higher in dogs found unowned, but it was low in dogs from friends and relatives, or from shelters, or home-bred.

So as in show business, in understanding these astonishingly complex and sensitive creatures and bringing them up happily, the key is timing. And the times given here are generally applicable, but different breeds of dogs can have different timing based on genetics, and so can individual dogs of the same breed, based more on matters beyond genetics. And since no two dogs can have exactly identical experiences in their first twelve weeks, every dog is a different personality, shaped by a panoply of factors we are just beginning to understand.

In the meantime, parents of human puppies may see some parallels here.

DING SUBMITS FOR A STOMACH RUB

*Chapter Eight*

# Dog Senses

The following declarations have been taken as fact by many people about the five (or six?) senses of dogs:

- Dogs like, no, they *love* to be touched, patted on the head, stroked.
- They'll eat anything, even the most disgusting stuff, and they wolf down meat—probably without tasting it.
- A dog's sense of smell is a million or even ten million times more acute than that of a human being.
- Dogs see in black and white. Everybody knows that. To a dog, the world looks like an Ansel Adams photograph, and not what you would expect in *National Geographic.*
- Dogs can hear sounds that don't register on the human ear–brain connection.
- Some dogs have ESP.

Well, not exactly.

# Touch

Touch is the earliest and maybe, according to some veterinarians, the most important of all the canine senses. The mother's touch—her mouth, her body, her teats—and the comradely feel of littermates all soothe the newborn pup and are crucial to the development of a mature mind. Puppies deprived of being touched by warm littermates or humans will usually turn out to be fearful, unaffectionate, and withdrawn.

The importance of touch to the dog is not all that difficult for a human to understand. Being touched, after all, is essential for human babies and is one of the great feel-good situations for human adults, be it motivated by affection or professional massage therapy. Throughout its life, a dog's greatest reward (except for those trained with food rewards) is to be stroked. Not only does it simply feel good, but it can lower the dog's heart rate and blood pressure and drop its skin temperature. (On the other hand, to return to our Navajo dog, wherever we touch him, he seems to heat up slightly under our fingers.) The calming effect seems to be a two-way street. Many studies have shown that if you stroke your dog, your blood pressure goes down and what is called your "state of arousal" lessens. Studies probably do not need to be undertaken to find out what happens to your blood pressure when, without warning, your dog barks.

Where dogs and humans vary deeply in the sense of touch is in the matter of fur. The hairs of a dog's covering of fur have been compared to levers—easily moved at the tip, with amplified effect at the base of the hair where the touch receptors are. Some areas of a dog's body are more sensitive to touch than others, the result of more or fewer touch receptor nerves. The muzzle and lips are especially sensitive, and the foot pads have specialized nerves that react to vibration, which let the animal know how stable the surface is on which he is moving. The spaces between the foot pads are highly sensitive, which is why many dogs intensely dislike being touched around the feet, something which dogs hardly ever do to one another.

Then, of course, there are whiskers. Technically called vibrissae, they are better thought of as antennae or feelers. Stiffer than hairs and longer, they are far more powerful "levers." At the base of each vibrissa lies a higher concentration of touch receptor cells than anywhere else on the dog's body. Indeed, almost half of the area of a dog's brain that is involved in touch is lit up by touches to the face, and in particular the upper jaw where the vibrissae are. They play a surprisingly important role, letting the dog know when potentially dangerous things are getting too close to the dog's face in dim light or darkness. Even the air currents pushed back at the dog as it nears a wall will push the vibrissae and warn the dog something is nearby. Also they help the dog find things near his mouth that his eyes cannot focus on. Trimming the vibrissae off, on the assumption that they are not important, is still practiced by some groomers, especially on show dogs. The practice is stressful for the dog and removes, at least temporarily, one of its ways of sensing its world.

One of the more woeful arguments about how dogs sense their world revolves around the notion of pain. Some people will tell you that dogs and other animals do not feel pain, at least in the sense that we do. The argument, made by some philosophers even today, suggests that dogs do not have self-awareness or consciousness like humans and therefore they are not conscious of pain. They are thus animate machines, a notion that excuses cruelty to them. Most people who have ever owned a dog know that this notion is ridiculous on its face. Dogs do have all the neural equipment for feeling pain that we humans do, and if it is not involved in feeling pain, what could it be for? Pain is very useful: it tells you to stop doing something that is harming you before it injures you seriously or kills you. Injured dogs limp, and yelp when hurt, just as you or I do. If it looks like pain, acts like pain, and sounds like pain, a wise philosopher would probably conclude that it is pain. Chronic pain, as in arthritis, is known to depress a dog's immune system (not to mention the dog itself), though most dogs are more stoic about pain than most humans.

Finally, on the sense of touch, evidence exists that men typically pet dogs differently than women—that is, a bit more roughly or, a man might say, more heartily. And, depending on their size, dogs don't like it all that much. Probably the best way to determine what kind of human touch is best for a dog is to think of what is most pleasant or unpleasant for a human. How many people do you know who just love being patted heartily on the head? And a lot of dogs, however affectionate they are, don't like to be hugged: it may makes them feel like they are being restrained, rather than adored. It's easy to tell if they don't like being hugged, they try to get away.

## Taste

Because something tastes good to humans does not mean it tastes good (or tastes at all) to a dog. Dogs are carnivores and not surprisingly they prefer meat to vegetables. Back in the 1970s, Katherine Houpt of Cornell University researched dogs' meat preferences. They are, in order: beef, pork, lamb, chicken, and horsemeat. They prefer canned or semimoist food to dry food and, oddly enough, they prefer their meat cooked.

The dog's progenitor, the wolf, is not as wedded to meat as are the cats (whom scientists sometimes refer to as "obligate" flesh eaters), but given the choice, wolves will stick to meat. At some point in the early domestication of the dog, which we assume took place in the garbage dumps of early villages, dogs had to have grown somewhat more catholic in their food preferences, in what they found palatable, palatability being defined no doubt by taste, smell, and texture. Wolves have little choice as far as palatability is concerned. They have to eat whatever they can kill.

So overall, the process of domestication has led to what can be thought of as more cosmopolitan if not necessarily more refined tastes. It is no doubt at these primordial garbage dumps that village dogs took to eating excrement when pressed, a habit that continues today, particularly among homeless dogs and also dogs who share space with horses and other herbivores whose digestion leaves plenty of nutrition in their droppings. Why dogs eat canine droppings including their own remains mysterious (and horrid for most dog lovers to contemplate). Another mystery is why dogs will occasionally eat grass. Like many people, I was taught that it was an emetic that got rid of food that was making the dog nauseated, but other suggestions have arisen. Grass might contain nutrients that a typical dog diet misses out on, or it could serve as a way of sweeping out internal parasites. So far, there is no reliable evidence for any of this.

Not surprisingly, if a puppy is given a variety of foods, it will be an adventurous eater as an adult, happily adjusting to new foods, same as with human children. Studies by pet nutritionists of beagles, Chow chows, poodles and others show that the reverse is also true. Puppies fed only soya beans would later eat no novel food. If fed a mixed vegetarian diet they would not eat meat. (This probably comes as no surprise to parents of human children.) Experience plays a considerable role in food preferences, possibly even the taste of the amniotic fluid in which the fetus dwells, and probably the flavors of the mother's milk which change depending on what the mother eats. But a good deal of canine food preferences appear to be genetic.

The typical human has about 9,000 taste buds; a dog has less than 2,000. So a dog's sense of taste cannot be anywhere near as acute or subtle. Not only that, dogs differ from other mammals in not having any taste buds that respond to salt (which is one of the four horsemen of human taste, the other three being sweet, sour, and bitter). Dogs respond to sugars (sucrose and fructose) and other sweet-tasting things. Cats, on the other hand, do not respond to sugars at all. As obligate carnivores, what use would sugars be to a cat, while many canids including domestic dogs will eat ripe fruit, a great and sweet source of energy. Dogs tend to be repelled by sour or bitter things.

Some breeds of dogs, like beagles, foxhounds, and Labrador retrievers will "wolf" down their food and eat a great deal at a sitting. Others, including some of the toy breeds, tend to be so fussy about food that it is hard to maintain their optimal weight. And individual dogs within breeds can differ in food preferences, as in just about everything else. Not many dogs, however, will avoid overeating given the opportunity, and some breeds (like the Lab) are famously gluttonous. Indeed, keeping one's pet dog from becoming overweight is, for many owners, an unending struggle.

# Smell

The sense of smell, of course, plays a major role in "tasting" the flavors of food. Dogs without a sense of smell were found to be unable to taste any differences in kinds of meat. But dogs without their sense of smell would hardly qualify as dogs, so central is it to their lives and, to us, so unimaginably powerful.

First, the smelling apparatus. Start at the tip of the nose, the black (or in some breeds brown or even pink) and usually cold and wet part called the leather. Dogs can move one nostril at a time, permitting them to sense the direction from which a scent is coming. The leather is moist with mucus from numerous glands, the molecules of scent attaching to the mucus and dissolving. Inside, little hairs push the dissolved scent back into the rest of the nose. The whole nose, of course, dominates the face of most breeds, a long, somewhat tubular scent-sensing tool. A beagle's nose contains about sixty square inches of flesh (epithelium) given over to sensing scents. That's an area as big as a standard piece of typing paper. By contrast, a human's olfactory epithelium has an area about the size of a postage stamp. The dog's olfactory epithelium is stretched over a series of bony plates and, again, in a beagle, it contains 225 million scent receptors. The champion scent hound, the bloodhound, has about 300 million scent receptors, while the diminutive dachshund has 125 million. A typical human has about five million receptors—2 percent of what a beagle has.

In a dog's nasal passage there is a kind of shelf, and when the dog sniffs, it draws the scent molecules up over the shelf where they can accumulate. When the dog breathes in or out or pants, the air passes below the shelf. Meanwhile the dog's receptors are sorting through the scent molecules which, of course, usually represent multiple scents. The receptors then send electrical signals to the brain, and two structures in the lower part of the back of the brain sort out all the different scents and the information they carry. The two structures are called olfactory bulbs, and those of a dog are about four times larger than a human's, two ounces in weight to a human's half ounce. And since a dog's brain is typically about one tenth the size of a human brain, the dog's brain devotes about forty times more of its brain to scent than the human brain does. When a dog is sniffing animal scents (to which it is especially attuned, having descended from hunters and still up to a hunt in many cases), it can be a million times more acute than a human. It can identify scents in such low concentration they approach that of homeopathic medicines which are below the concentrations that even the most sensitive scientific equipment can pick up.

What is more, humans are likely to sense just one scent at a time—whichever one is strongest; a dog can sort through numerous scents that are simultaneously in its nose, separating one from another and "responding" mentally to each. If we smell a stew cooking, a dog smells each ingredient of the stew, along with the bread warming up and the red wine breathing on the sideboard, not to mention the cook and the fact that the cat walked past the stove five minutes ago. This analogy, for which I am largely indebted to Stanley Coren, is perhaps the best way to begin to imagine what it might be like to smell as acutely as a dog.

What does this astounding olfactory acuity permit the dog to do? As early as 1895, an investigator named G. J. Romanes attempted to test it. He set off at the head of a single-file procession of twelve men. Each man was careful to step in the footprints of those who preceded him. After some distance, the column split in two, each half heading off in a different direction. Then Romanes's dog was brought to the starting point and, at the split, unhesitatingly followed the six men led by Romanes. Dogs have shown that they can discriminate between identical twins in separate tracking tests, but if given the scent of one twin and then a track by the other, they will follow the track of the wrong twin. So the dog's olfactory acuity operates with twins much as humans' vision does. It's hard for most people to tell the difference between identical twins unless the two are fairly close together. Ultimately, a world dominated by thousands of scents is unfathomable to the human mind, which is operated by a neural system that is as given over to vision as the dog's neural system is to smell.

## Sight

The common wisdom is that somehow dogs sacrificed acute vision for sensational olfactory talents; dogs are said not to see very well. Certainly they don't see the world the way we do. To begin with, they look out on the world from about fifteen or twenty inches above the ground. Creep around your house for a few minutes on your knees and you will see the world at a dog's *angle*. While you're at it, creep up close to an adult—close enough, say, to be patted heartily on the head—squint your eyes hard, and look up at the person. If your squint has made your vision a little blurry, what you see is pretty close to what you look like to a dog.

In some breeds of dog, the nose and the rest of the face have been so flattened that the eyes face almost forward, a bit like us humans and apes. We have a wide swath of what is called binocular vision, which is to say a wide range in which we see the same object with both eyes, thus perceiving depth, distance. Flat-faced dogs and sight-hound breeds like Afghans and Salukis have some binocular vision, though not as wide a swath as we do. But for most dogs, the eyes are set wider apart, which provides a very narrow range of binocular vision, so narrow that such a dog cannot really see something that lies a inch or two in front of its nose. On the other hand, the lack of binocular vision is matched by much greater (wider) lateral vision. Dogs have a far greater area of peripheral (nonbinocular) vision than we do, capable of seeing quite far toward the rear of their heads.

The details of the dog's eye came about in response to what, in its niche, the dog needed to see, just as its tolerance for various kinds of food came about in response to life in the village dump. And before that, of course, there were wolves (who have more lateral vision than most dogs, by the way). A lot of prey animals are particularly active at dawn and sunset. They are what is called crepuscular, so it would pay for a predator (like a wolf) to be able to see well in dim light. It would be helpful to see distant herds on the horizon with some acuity, and it would be crucial to see when they moved, when they ran.

The first thing to notice about a dog's eye is that its black center, the pupil, is very large. The pupil is what gathers light into the eye and the larger the pupil, the more light it collects. If you think of it in the terms of a camera—the kind with film, remember them?—the pupil deals with "aperture." If you are photographing in bright light you want a high f-stop, like f/22, practically a pinhole—to let in just a little bit of the glare. But if you are photographing in very low light, you want to achieve a really low f-stop, like f/2, meaning the lens on the camera is wide open. So the canine pupil evolved to be large, to let in a lot of what light is available during darker times of the day.

The light passes through the transparent cornea and through the pupil to the lens which sits right inside the iris, the colored part of the eye. In an eye, it is the iris that closes down or opens up the pupil. The cornea plays a role in focusing the light that enters the eye, but the main focusing feature is, of course, the lens. The lens is attended by muscles which can change its shape, a process called accommodation. As a human ages, the lens becomes stiff and the muscles that change its shape weaken, making it harder to focus—one reason why so many older people wear glasses. A dog's lens, which is bigger than a human's, accommodates about as well as a septuagenarian's—not very well.

The lens refracts (bends) incoming light and concentrates it onto the retina that lies at the back of the eyeball. The retina is equivalent to the film in the camera. It is the place that receives the image carried by the light that is focused by the lens. If the cornea and lens are the right configuration—that is, the right power for bending light—the image that reaches the retina will be sharp and in focus. If the lens is too powerful, it focuses the light prematurely, a little bit inside the retina, and the image will be blurred. This is called nearsightedness, and there are breeds of dogs that tend to be nearsighted, suggesting that it is a genetic disorder. In a test of several breeds, more than half of German shepherds, Rottweilers, and schnauzers were found to be nearsighted. On the other hand, retriever breeds were found to have a high frequency of mild farsightedness—which is when the lens is too weak, and bends the incoming light at an angle where it would focus *beyond* the retina. Most dog breeds, it turns out, suffer from neither near- nor farsightedness. But they do not see most details as clearly as humans do, and that is because the dog retina is structured to work best in low light.

That old-fashioned item, film, is covered with an emulsion containing silver grains which undergo a chemical reaction when struck by light. In low light, it is best to have a film that has relatively large grains, since they will be more likely to be struck by rays of light than smaller ones. This tends to make a grainy photograph. In bright light, you want a film with smaller grains so that you can maximize the amount of detail in the resulting photograph. But retinas aren't interchangeable, so a retina—human or canine—is going to have to be a compromise of some sort. For the human, the compromise is tilted toward daylight; for dogs it tilts to low light.

The human retina ("designed" for maximum acuity in daylight) has two kinds of light receptors, rods and cones, that are named for their shape. The rods collect light and report it to the brain as a gray scale, from very light gray to very dark gray. The cones collect light in various wavelengths that is perceived as color. Both the human and canine retina has both kinds of receptor cells, but the human eye has a greater proportion of cones than a dog's eye. The cones are, in a sense, the equivalent of very fine-grained color film. (So dogs *do* see in more than just black and white.) Cones tend to lie among little clusters of rods, but in the human eye, there is a place on the retina just in the line of sight—that is, directly back from the center of the pupil—that is made up entirely of cones. This is called the fovea, and it is the reason why humans can see such incredible detail in the world around us.

Dogs don't have foveas. And they have a majority of rods in little clusters, so their vision is necessarily grainy. And because their pupil is so big, it acts like a wide-open camera lens and reduces depth of field. If you are operating at a low f-stop, say f/2, and you focus on a champagne bottle on a table in a field, the champagne bottle will be in focus, the table will be a bit blurry, and the field will be just a featureless blur. Close down the aperture to a higher f-stop, say f/22, and everything will be in focus from the front edge of the table to infinity. Dogs cannot close down their pupil enough to put everything in focus in bright light. So dogs are operating with grainy vision and lousy depth of field.

Instead of a fovea, dogs do have an area in the same place that has more cones than rods, but they also have a horizontal streak of cones across the retina. Mammals that go fast typically have such a streak—antelopes and cheetahs, for example, are among those animals with the most pronounced streaks. The streak is believed to make things happening on the horizon, such as an approaching herd of elk, highly noticeable. In addition, the streak makes for high acuity when it comes to something moving. Dogs notice any motion within view, but they may not notice a still object.

Underneath the layer of receptor cells in a dog's eye is an opaque layer, the tapetum lucidum, that reflects light back into the rods and cones. This is what makes a dog's eyes shine greenish-yellow in the beam of headlights or flashlights.

All in all, then, the dog's eye is a holdover from the wolf's eye, designed for a low light world. Dogs do have good night vision. But except for coonhounds and bloodhounds and so forth (who are scent hounds), and some guard dogs, most dogs sleep at night and operate mostly during the day. Certainly that is the case for virtually all pet dogs. Then why haven't dogs' eyes evolved to be daytime eyes? Wouldn't they be better off with eyes like ours?

Evolution lesson: first of all, it is not just the eyes. The dog has those huge olfactory bulbs taking up skull space.

How would they fit another big interpretation center into their skulls? So a whole apparatus would have to come about, including a new schedule of development so that the skull could grow enough to accommodate the new neural apparatus. That would take a whole lot of evolving. But the real answer is simple. There is no need for such a thing. Dogs do fine with the visual system they inherited from wolves. A lot of village dog scavenging goes on at night or in the early morning, for example, so night vision would have been helpful at that stage of domestication. And since then there has been very little pressure on dogs—what biologists call selective pressure—to evolve a daytime visual system. Any domestic dogs that did have incrementally better daytime vision would not, for that reason, get to breed more than any other dog, because slightly better vision in daylight would probably go unnoticed by the owners, who arrange dog matings based on more noticeable traits. Or by dogs themselves, the males of which tend not to be fussy about mating partners. So the trait—slightly better day vision—would not be artificially or naturally selected for.

It is conceivable, in a science-fiction way, that modern equipment could be used to establish which dogs in a litter had a few more cones in their retinas, and select for them and see what happened, but my guess is that dogs who could smell as well as they do and could see all the detail they now cannot would go crazy in some unfortunate way from information overload and, if they survived, would not in fact be dogs anymore. Temple Grandin, an animal scientist who is also autistic, believes that dogs and most other animals are highly sensitive to details in their field of vision—so sensitive that they cannot "see the forest for the trees." In studies of autism, this is called "hyper-specificity." Grandin writes that animals lack the two large frontal lobes on their cortex that humans have, and that pull together all the information reaching the brain via the senses—that is, raw data—into schemas, into generalized views, into what she calls "the big picture." Dogs and other animals—along with many autistic people whose frontal lobes don't work perfectly—she holds, have to work with just raw data, "the tiny details that go into the picture."

Finally, as noted, it turns out that dogs can see color. Some color. The human eye has three kinds of cones. One kind responds to blue (short wavelengths of light), another to green (medium wavelengths) and the third to orange (long wavelengths). All three respond to incoming light and the combined activity can create all the colors of the rainbow in the mind. Dogs have fewer cones, so whatever color they see will not be as rich as what we can see. Also, they have only two types of cones: one is identical with our blue cone and one that seems to function at wavelengths somewhere between green and orange—something like yellow.

It has now been fairly well established by Jay Neitz and colleagues at the University of California at Santa Barbara that the dog's rainbow is dark blue, light blue, gray, light yellow, darker yellow, and dark gray. No reds. Anything green, yellow, or orange will appear yellowish. Red may appear as black. So, as Stanley Coren has pointed out, if you want to play Frisbee with your dog, don't get one that is blue—it will disappear against the blue sky. Get a yellow one and paint a dark blue bull's eye on it so when the dog misses and the Frisbee lands in the grass, it won't get lost there.

# Hearing

A larger fraction of a dog's brain is given over to making sense out of sounds than that of the human brain, even that of Mozart. Dogs can hear more sounds than we can, especially higher pitched ones. And they can also hear sounds that are quieter or farther away than we can. Not only that: most dogs can tell the direction a sound is coming from faster than we can—in as little as a six hundredth of a second.

All true.

Dogs' ears can, with some exceptions, turn toward an incoming sound, and can turn independently of each other. This is especially true of dogs with prick ears—that is, erect ears like German shepherds' and wolves' ears, which are especially good at determining the directionality of sounds.

But first, what exactly is an incoming sound? The answer is changes in air pressure that are picked up by ears and turned into nervous signals that reach the brain. So does the tree falling in the middle of the jungle make a sound? No, it makes changes in air pressure which go unfulfilled unless there are ears in the neighborhood. The changes in air pressure typically emanate in the form of waves, increasing and then decreasing many times per second. How many times the wave cycles from high to low in one second is called its frequency, and is measured in hertz (Hz), which simply means cycles per second. Higher frequency waves are heard as higher pitch and, conversely, lower frequency waves are heard as lower pitch. Healthy young humans can hear from about 20Hz (which is something like the lowest note the bass player can make) to 20,000Hz (which would be about three octaves above the high notes on a piano). Waves with lower frequencies than about 20Hz cannot be heard but can be felt as physical vibrations, and are collectively called infrasound. Waves with frequencies too high for humans to hear are called ultrasound. Human hearing is most acute at around 2,000Hz, which is the frequency of most human speech—spoken language playing perhaps the key role in the evolution of modern human beings.

The lowest frequencies a dog can hear are similar to those of humans, plus or minus a few hertz. But dogs can hear much higher notes, frequencies of about 40,000Hz. Many of the wild canids, including wolves in some places and seasons, rely for food upon small rodents—mice, voles, and so forth. These creatures mostly communicate in ultrasound—high-pitched little squeaks—and it is critical that the canids be able to hear them; hence, the domestic dog's hearing ability. Cats, who rely far more on the likes of mice for food, can hear up to 45,000Hz. Bats, who use ultrasound to echolocate (like a submarine's sonar), operate in the range of 30,000 to about 100,000Hz.

Ultrasound can also be an enemy of the dog's ear. I noticed years ago that whenever I began to vacuum the rugs in the house, the dogs all left, slinking out of sight as fast as they could. My explanation was that often when engaged in this chore I find myself swearing because of tangled electrical cords or chairs that are obstinately in my way and the dogs figured I was swearing at them for some unknowable reason. But no. Some vacuum cleaners emit loud ultrasonic shrieks that make the dogs uncomfortable, as do electric drills and other tools.

Frequency is one thing; intensity or loudness is another. Loudness is measured in decibels, zero decibels being the lower limit of human ability to hear a sound, either because it is very quiet or very far away. A hundred or so decibels denotes a sound that is painfully loud for a human, easily capable of damaging human ears. Rock music and its ever louder successors have prematurely deafened millions of people, young and old, and very likely has the same effect on dogs' ears. Hunters' organizations have recently begun to warn their members about firing their shotguns too close to their hunting dogs' ears. Dogs can hear sounds that are far quieter than anything humans can hear—some estimates say dogs' acuteness is twice ours, other estimates rise to five times more than ours. One can only imagine what a shotgun, exploding within a few feet of a dog's ears, must sound like.

The dog's ears, like the ears of wolves, jackals, and foxes, are attuned to hear the slightest rustling of grass when a little creature is moving about some fifty yards away. On the other hand, it remains possible that dogs can screen out a lot of sounds that, to them, signify nothing, just as puppies learn not to overreact to meaningless loud sounds. I have the sense that none of our six dogs hears anything meaningful from a television set except for the occasional barking of a dog, or the howling of a wolf or coyote on some nature program. They may just screen out most of human electronic culture—not all that insignificant a talent.

## ESP

A huge anecdotal literature exists about dogs exhibiting startling powers—such as knowing within minutes of when their owners are coming home and going to camp out at the front door, or, along with farm animals, predicting by bizarre behavior the imminence of earthquakes, or getting left behind and traveling across an entire continent, fording streams, heading off attacks by mountain lions, avoiding speeding semis while crossing superhighways, to find themselves, bedraggled, exhausted but happy on their owners' doorsteps a year later. These stories and others like them often give rise to the notion that dogs have ESP—extrasensory perception.

In the first place, dogs are subject to what are called body rhythms, most notably a circadian rhythm, meaning twenty-four hours, as are many other creatures. In fact, some dogs have a twenty-hour circadian rhythm, others twenty-two, still others twenty-four. In any event, studies have shown that some dogs can be trained to react within one minute's accuracy to an event that occurs every twenty-four hours. So it is not exactly extrasensory perception, but instead a matter of learning about the passage of time. Some such events are harder to explain, however, including the story of a Husky named Sascha who belonged to a friend of ours who owned a bookstore. He would take the Husky to the bookstore each day, but then the store moved to a venue where dogs were not permitted. So he left the dog home and she would escape and go to the old bookstore, crossing highways on the way, and this was deemed too dangerous. So Sascha was boarded during the day with us (we worked at home) and her owner would pick her up within fifteen minutes of the store's closing. About ten minutes before her owner turned up, Sascha would be waiting at the front door.

But then her owner was given a job in Hawaii and Sascha was deemed too old to survive the six months of quarantine that state demands. So Sascha was left with us and our dogs. She soon realized that her owner was not going to show up and gave up her vigil at the door. Then one weekend about six months later, Sascha returned to her vigil at the front door, giving it up after the weekend. We discovered several weeks later that her owner had returned to town for that very weekend but had not wanted to stir things up emotionally (for himself mainly) by coming by to see his dog. This is very difficult to explain. How could that old dog sense that her owner was somewhere in town on the few days that he was?

The great ethologist, Niko Tinbergen, said that ESP simply refers to something that is beyond the known senses or beyond the known senses' capabilities, adding that until recently no one knew that bats echolocate and elephants communicate in infrasound. So who is to say?

Many geologists are fascinated by the activities of dogs, horses, cows, pigs, and the like, who often go a bit nutty before earthquakes—or at least some earthquakes. Chinese seismologists evacuated the city of Haicheng in 1975 because animals were acting up—and a huge quake leveled the city the next day. As many as a million lives were saved. On the other hand, a bit later, a quake took another Chinese city and its animals totally by surprise and nearly a million people perished. What is going on in such occasional circumstances remains unknown. Some scientists suggest that it could have something to do with magnetic interruptions in the earth, ultrasound, or maybe electromagnetic disturbances in the atmosphere. No one knows, and very few seismologists have bothered to find out, relying more on instrumentation that is also of nearly unimaginable sensitivity.

As for those dogs who find their way home à la *The Incredible Journey*, one explanation often offered is that they can navigate by the angle of the sun's rays, or the polarization of light or some kind of electromagnetic sense. Again, there is no explanation that people can agree upon. But in this regard, it is important to point out that probably for each such tale, a thousand or more dogs wander off, get lost, and never do find their way home.

JUPITER COLLECTS EGGS. HERE, HE GROWLS AT A HEN WHO
DOESN'T UNDERSTAND DOG LANGUAGE.

## Chapter Nine

# Communication

Dogs bark, God knows. Except for the (blessedly) barkless Basenjis, all breeds of dog bark, a little or a lot. According to the cartoonist Gary Larson, whose work is most often taped to walls in biology departments, a barking dog is saying "Hey." Or, more often, "Hey, hey, hey, hey . . ."

In fact, a dog's "hey" is a bit more complicated than that acoustically, but it does mean essentially "hey." And, in fact, practically all mammals and birds bark. This was discovered in the 1970s by ornithologist Gene Morton during the heyday of zoological research at the Smithsonian's National Zoological Park. Morton had a widowed Carolina wren in his office and grew curious about the *chirts* the bird emitted from time to time. The *chirts* were known to function as an alert, an alarm call. So he made sonograms, or voice prints, of them and found that the Carolina wren's basic *chirt* showed up on paper as a chevron, an inverted V.

It is an axiom of biology that the form of something (like a leg or a beak or a nose) follows or embodies its function. So the sound of the wren's alert—its form—was a chevron. He then looked into the alarm or alert calls of other birds and mammals, a task rendered pretty simple by being at a zoo. It turned out that such alert calls as the bark of a dog and the alarm calls of some seventy-five bird and mammal species also were in the form of a chevron.

What the chevron shows is that the wren's or dog's voice goes up, then down, and it happens so fast that the human ear hears it as one abrupt chirt or bark. What is the function of an ascending sound, and what is the function of a descending sound? A high-pitched dog whine generally signals that the dog is distressed, perhaps afraid. If it is a puppy, the whine means it is afraid, distressed, or hungry. On the other hand, a low growl means the dog is aggressive, annoyed, threatening. A whine appears as a thin line in the upper part of the sonogram, a growl as a rougher line at the bottom. A harsh snarl, part of an aggressive bite perhaps, appears as a blotchy thick line. A harsh squeal, perhaps leading to a fear bite, appears in the upper part as a blotchy line.

In a sense, up is a babyish sound, like puppies whining for their supper. In an adult, it signifies fearfulness, submission: "Don't hurt me, I'm little" and also "I am not going to attack you." Conversely, the growl is clearly a threat, and the loud snarl may well mean you're about to be bitten. Humans share this basic pattern. Dog owners, for example, will rarely tell their dog to come and sit in an ascending, high-pitched voice. Nor do most humans address infant children in a descending voice. And is it not true that people universally end a question with an ascending question mark?

So what does the chevron-shaped bark represent, being a

little bit up and then a little bit down? Basically, it is a two-part "Hey." It says, "Uh oh, what's that?" and then "Whatever it is, I am alert to its presence." A tiny tinge of uncertainty and fear is followed by a resolute statement of readiness and this, as noted, is a bit more complicated than Larson's "Hey."

Morton called all this the Motivational-Structural rules: each sound has a particular structure, and the structure is directly tied to what is motivating the animal. The sounds express the animal's state of mind at the moment—which is to say its emotions. Descended from wolves, the dog's vocal repertoire is little different from wolves in kind, though quite different in usage. For example, adult wolves do bark, but typically as a warning, presumably to the pack, when something or someone untoward is noticed. Mech reports that wolf puppies, on the other hand, are frequent barkers. Possibly, adult dogs have retained the wolf puppy's penchant for barking, another example of neoteny in the process of domestication. Dogs that yapped a lot when approached by nocturnal strangers might well have been favored over those who lay low.

Other researchers into the acoustics of dog barking have found that the "uh oh, what's that" bark tends to be noisy and atonal. On the other hand, when a dog is having a positive time—when it is playing, for example—its bark will be more musical. In a stranger-is-at-the-door scenario, the dog's barks are usually low-pitched and rapidly repeated. Isolation barks are apt to be high-pitched and come one at a time. (Our Navajo dog, when caught on the wrong side of the door, emits a wimpy, yelp-like pair of barks, over and over like the Chinese water torture, until someone opens the door. Thus has he trained us. Quite the opposite, though with the same effect, when Teacup the Hopi dog wants to come in, she emits a quiet "wuff" and waits patiently, then wuffs again. Susanne taught Teacup to whisper by giving her a dog biscuit when she succeeded. Now sometimes she will whisper in hopes of getting a dog biscuit, which brings all the other dogs from far and wide, hoping for the same thing.)

Some students of barking point out that it is only dogs—among all the wild canids—who bark often and in varying tonalities depending on the situation at hand. This, it is speculated, came about because it turned out to be a fairly effective way for dogs to communicate less to each other than to humans.

As noted in the chapter on puppies, they tend to yelp when cold, hurt, hungry, or too far from the den. This is a very effective form of communication, for not only does it let the mother know that something is up that may need her attention. The yelp also stimulates her brain to pass the information along to the pituitary gland, which in turn causes the release of the hormone oxytocin, which in turn causes her mammary glands to let milk flow—in all, an automatic cascade of useful physical events proceeding from an acoustical signal.

Adult dogs retain another childish trait in that they whine, but you hardly ever hear an adult dog whining at another unless it is trying to show complete submission to a dominant dog. Often they direct a whine at us humans. That whining is a great attention-getter is learned by most puppies. They continue its use as adults to get human attention. It is, in this situation, a learned response (and can presumably be discouraged by not responding to it).

Wolves are famous for howling, which serves a number of purposes, mainly to call the pack together, to advertise the pack's territory to potential interlopers, and to rev the pack up for the hunt. As David Mech noted, there are loneliness howls, pass-the-alarm-down-the-line howls, and let's-celebrate howls. It has been found that when approaching the source of a stranger's howl, a wolf howls in a lower pitch than usual. On the other hand, dogs rarely howl, and in most cases only when left behind, using the howl to try to call in the pack—i.e., the pet's family members. Huskies, Malamutes, pack hounds, and Dobermans are more given to howling than most other dogs, with the hounds baying for other reasons than abandonment— a kind of cheerleading, perhaps. Our Navajo dog, whose father was a big Doberman, starts howling when he sees my wife and me drive off, instigating a group howl that goes on for about four minutes, then for some reason coming to a halt. Another curiosity is how many dogs will howl along with certain kinds of music—is the dog actually trying to sing along or is it just howling for the fun of it? No one knows exactly what is going on in such bouts.

Howling is, of course, a long-distance communication for the most part: the Motivational-Structural rules (what can loosely be called the Growl and Whine school) apply chiefly to close-up communications. Gene Morton of the National Zoo presented the Growl and Whine rules as a hypothesis, based on careful observation and collection of facts. But a scientific hypothesis is of no use if it doesn't make predictions that can be shown to be true or (equally important) false. One prediction was that the greater a species' social complexity, the more complete the range of sound qualities that will be expressed. In other words, along the acoustic continuum from growl to whine, with the bark a kind of midpoint, a social animal would have more different sounds than a loner. That is because a more complex social life would require a more subtle expression of an animal's mood.

Fortunately, the National Zoo at the time had examples of three South American canids, two of whom we met in chapter two. The maned wolf, which most likely evolved from some sort of fox and not wolves, is a loner, remaining by itself except to mate. The bush dog, on the other hand, is highly gregarious and lives and hunts in packs. Third is the crab-eating fox, who lives in pairs but evidently hunts alone. Like all other wild canids, these three have in common the classic whine and growl vocalizations. Morton found that in all three, infant whines elicit care from parents and protest rough treatment. The adult crab-eating fox and the maned wolf also use the whine as a sign of submission.

But the bush dog has elaborated the whine into a complex string of distinct sounds corresponding to different states of arousal. They go from a simple one-syllable whine, to various collections of whine syllables, to a fusion of whine syllables into a whine-scream. The bush dogs' repetitive whines are used in food sharing and most other situations requiring group contact, and also let each member of the pack know where the others are—useful for a species that lives much of the time in dense foliage. The bush dogs also growl when a hostile or unfamiliar individual gets too close, as do the maned wolf and the crab-eating fox, both of which also bark as a warning. Bush dogs only bark when they are mad at each other.

Most of the vocalizations of the bush dogs, then, tend to the high side and are what might be called affiliative, keeping the pack in touch and together. On the opposite extreme, most of the maned wolf's vocalizations are harsh, on the lower side, fewer in kind, and designed to maintain distance between individuals.

A nifty bit of evolutionary logic lies behind Morton's Motivational-Structural rules. Consider the frog, say a big male, croaking in the night at the edge of a pond. You can tell he is big by the basso profundo croak. Frogs and other amphibians and many reptiles continue to grow until their death. And the bigger a frog gets, the lower its croak is in pitch. Female frogs, looking for male frog excellence, go for the biggest, deepest-voiced, oldest, and therefore most certainly successful male. And younger, smaller males are not likely to challenge the big male for females or territory or anything else.

Along come the birds and mammals. They do not grow throughout life but, instead reach a genetically prearranged adult size and stop growing. Many mammals are nocturnal and many birds live in fairly dense forest habitats, meaning that they are not easily seen. In such a situation it is a great advantage for a bird or a mammal to *sound like* it is the biggest on the block—hence, the low growl that virtually all birds and mammals are capable of. A low threatening growl is often a sufficient deterrent to an intruder into one's territory. Similarly, a whine suggesting that the whiner is not interested in attacking (seeming smaller) is another way of avoiding fights, which are energy-consuming and dangerous.

Of course, many mammals, including most canids, are diurnal, and they also have an interest in seeming bigger, which is accomplished by raising their hackles when threatening another animal. Body language in dogs is complex (though not as complex as that of wolves), and its meanings are usually clear to other dogs, though human intervention and some of the unintended consequences of domestication—docked or curled tails, for example—have rendered dog body language less expressive than that of wolves, and also sometimes ambiguous.

One of the more powerful nonvocal signals in dogs (most anyway) is the simple act of staring. Dominant dogs stare down less dominant ones. If the less dominant dog continues to stare back, it may get snarled at or bitten. A submissive dog avoids direct eye contact altogether, turning away. Border collies are famous for giving "eye" to the sheep, staring them into psychological submission. (Dogs tend to watch us by watching our eyes: a dog owner should probably insist on staring down the dog, lest it get uppity in other ways. I do that if I remember to.) Other ways that dogs demonstrate dominance over one another is—just as with wolves—to stand tall with tail up and head up, perhaps putting the head over the body of the weaker one, and with the ears pricked. This latter signal is not available to floppy-eared breeds. If the dominant dog is in a high state of aggression, it will also curl its lips back revealing its teeth, and raise its hackles.

A submissive dog will try to look smaller, by holding its head and body low, the ears flat against its head, and the tail held down, close to the body. If the dog is not only submissive but fearful, it will cringe, put its tail between its legs, even roll over on its back and, if really scared, pee on itself. A dog that needs to make it absolutely clear that it poses no threat will roll over on its back and sometimes wag its tail happily. Many pet dogs do this when their owner walks in the room. Raymond Coppinger, the biologist, sneered at such behavior, saying that he—as a raiser of sled dogs and herding dogs—didn't want them all rolling around on the floor every time he came upon them, so he discouraged it. Many pet owners, on the other hand, take this behavior as an invitation to rub the dog's stomach—which, of course, the dog loves. I think that a lot of this rolling over, exposing the stomach and the crotch area, while indicating submission to a dominant dog, has also been learned by each successive generation of dogs to be a way to get a human to scratch its stomach. After all, it is likely that the human smile evolved from a signal to a stranger that you mean no harm to an expression of pleasure shared between friends or acquaintances. How different is that from a submissive posture ("I mean you no harm") to the equivalent of a smile? By the way, dogs have arguably learned to smile, pulling the corners of their mouths way back, revealing their teeth, with their mouths open, doing so in circumstances in human-dog relations when a smile is altogether appropriate.

A dog that is mainly just scared may assume a posture that is part snarl, part cringe. This is when most dog bites—called fear-bites—occur. Veterinarians are especially tuned to this since they must handle strange and typically fearful dogs all day. Many people, including most children, have no idea about these signals of fear, and proceed to invade the space of a fearful dog, often with tragic results. Usually a change in mood from calmness or submission to fear can be read in the gradual change in the dog's posture, but some breeds like Rottweilers (and some individual dogs of any breed or mixture of breeds) can be poor at providing body signals and go straight from calm to a fear-bite.

Of all the visual signals dogs make, those made with the tail are perhaps the most clearly expressive. A tail that is rapidly swishing back and forth or revolving like a propeller means, essentially, happiness and excitement. A tail that is held erect, switching back and forth at the top, is a sign of annoyance (same as a housecat) and usually a prelude to a threat. During an attack the tail is typically held straight out horizontally. A dog signaling complete submission may wag its tail down low or even between its legs. A dog's tail is something of an amplifier, adding to the information embodied in the body's positions and in facial expressions. Dogs with docked tails are thus more likely to be misunderstood, particularly at a distance. And think of the disadvantages of being an Old English sheepdog: not only is its tail typically docked, but it has been designed so that its hair hangs down over its eyes. In essence, it has been blinded and given the equivalent of a speech impediment.

For a dog, appearances can be deceiving, however, while scent is its most highly refined sensory capacity. Consider a one hundred and eighty-pound mastiff seeing its first Pekingese. There is no particular reason why the mastiff would see the tiny creature as another dog, but its scent would clearly and certainly say "dog." Dogs fill the world with a cornucopia of scents, called pheromones, and these scents provide specific information about the dog's identity, age, sexual and social status, and emotional and physiological state. The pheromones issue forth from a large collection of glands here and there around the body, particularly on the head, feet, and rear end. The most important of these are the anal glands, located on either side of the anus. In these glands are various bacteria and an active process of fermentation which, taken together, produce probably a dozen or so different scents. When dogs greet each other, they first sniff the anal region and usually move on to sniff each others' lips, thus developing an olfactory "view" of each others' identity and state of being. It is presumed that pheromones operate on the sniffer's mood in a subliminal way.

Feces and urine are carriers of pheromones and leave identifying information in place, and dogs—particularly male dogs—use both to mark their territories. Dogs often scratch the ground around their feces or urine, an act most people see as some vestigial attempt at covering it up, but it seems more likely that the scratching simply acts to call more attention to the message. Most male dogs learn to lift their hind legs when urinating, the better to leave the message at nose level. The higher up one urinates, the bigger and thus more dominant one seems. A male will typically cover another male's urine and that of a female who is going into heat. Females do not scent-mark as frequently as males, but often visit scent posts near home; when in estrus they wander more widely and scent-mark more often, spreading the good news around.

A female unwittingly uses scent-marking in a deceptive manner, sending out the message that she is ready for sex a week or so before she reaches estrus and ovulates. This is likely to increase the number of males attracted to her, leading to competition among the males with the likely result that the female will wind up mating with the fittest male.

It is highly likely that many pet dogs' seeming ability to read their owners' mood is a matter of scent. Certainly the remarkably sensitive olfactory abilities of dogs—the equivalent of sensing a single grain of salt dissolved in a family-sized swimming pool—are responsible for an astounding medical feat in which a dog kept sniffing at its owner's leg frequently enough that she had it the spot examined by a doctor who found an incipient melanoma there and removed it, thus perhaps saving her life.

The acuteness and precision of a dog's sense of smell has led humans to train dogs to locate explosives and other contraband like drugs inside trucks and other containers, to find people caught in building collapses waiting to be rescued, to locate buried victims of murder, and a host of other things the odors of which defy the best human instruments. A California woman who operates a winery has taught her dog to sniff out any bottles in which the cork has gone bad, thus spoiling the wine.

So far at least, no machine has been devised that is as sensitive as a dog's nose.

Chapter Ten

# The Enigma of Play

Some 2,000 years ago, the Greek philosopher Plato took note of the common tendency among many animals, particularly young ones, to leap playfully into the air. He theorized from this and other observations that growing young animals, including humans, needed exercise the most and so they play the most, leading to the acquisition of endurance and those physical skills needed later as an adult. He went on to trace the origin of dance to the habitual play of animals.

In 1980, one of the pioneers in the scientific study of animal play, Robert Fagen, wrote that our "concept of play as physical training has not improved significantly in the two millennia since Plato."

In fact, until about the 1970s, most biological scientists sniffed at the notion of studying animal play because it seemed to be basically senseless behavior, indeed, "behavioral fat," as one scientist grumped. It was not the sort of thing that could be shown to have biological or evolutionary consequences (except bad ones like falling down and injuring oneself, all the while wasting needed energy). Another reason play was avoided by serious academics was that it is an anthropomorphism trap. To watch two ravens doing synchronized barrel rolls in the wind is to see two ravens having fun. Clearly a kitten batting a ball of yarn around the floor is enjoying itself. The exuberance of puppies running around and knocking each other over can hardly be different in kind than the exuberance of young boys doing the same thing.

But having fun was considered, for a very long time and in some quarters still today, a human emotion that cannot be attributed to lower animals. Or at least there was no scientific means of determining if a dog or a rat or even a chimpanzee possessed such emotions. So most students of animal behavior followed the path embarked on by B. F. Skinner and others (including Ivan Pavlov), studying conditioned responses of pigeons and the like. "Lower animals" are, of course, all nonplant creatures below humans on the great chain of being. The Great Chain of Being—a medieval concept of the world—led in a straight vertical line from horrid creepy-crawlies up to humans and beyond to angels and finally God. The complexities of evolution replaced the Chain more than a century ago, but many people still talk of the "lower" animals. This despite the certainty, based on the sheer numbers of species, that God clearly has what the great British biologist J. B. S. Haldane called "an inordinate fondness for beetles."

If animals had emotions, it was believed, they had to be simple urges—like aggression or fear, hunger, and sex. Such human-like emotions as happiness, affection, embarrassment, or fun were simply out of the question since animals did not possess the kind of self-awareness that psychologists and philosophers assume underlay such emotions. Animals, even those animals we humans had molded to rely upon us for their existence and to watch us very closely, like dogs, could neither suffer nor enjoy—except, of course, in an extremely primitive way, such as learning to salivate when Dr. Pavlov rang his bell. So animal play was deemed unimportant.

As late as the 1980s, an explanation for animal play arose called the Surplus Resource Theory, which postulated that animals, especially young ones who were well-fed and -cared for—either by assiduous wild parents or by pet owners or zoo keepers—would play to burn off excess energy. Domestic animals and zoo animals would be more likely to play than wild animals. This, of course, said that play was of no value in itself, but was merely a byproduct of good nutrition. (In fact, most studies of animal play have been carried out with captive or domesticated animals since they are far more easily kept within view.)

But even in the 1960s, it had become clear that animal play was very common. Most mammals do it, many birds do it, even one reptile was known to do it. This last was Pigface, a Nile soft-shelled turtle, who lived his life in an aquarium in the Smithsonian's National Zoological Park in Washington, D.C. Such turtles are considered to be among the brainiest of their kind and perhaps Pigface got bored, alone in his aquarium rather than patrolling the Nile, and he began scratching himself and other harmful stereotyped behavior. The keeper decided to give him a few toys, such as a soccer ball, and Pigface began to push the ball around with his nose. He later initiated a tug-of-war when the keeper placed a feeding tube in the water.

As it happens, a great deal has been found out about play

since Fagen published *Animal Play Behavior* in 1980, but it is fair to say that the subject remains a thicket of conceptual, philosophical, and biological disagreements. There isn't even a generally accepted scientific *definition* of play, though most students agree that there are three basic kinds of animal play. One is called locomotory—when an animal just runs around, stopping and starting and changing direction abruptly, rolls on the ground or, as Plato noted, leaps—a general enthusiastic cavorting.

Another form is object play, when the animal picks up a stick or some other object in its mouth and throws it into the air, chasing it. Or it leaps at a fuzzy animal toy, snatching it up and shaking it violently, later lying down to chew it to pieces. Fetching a ball thrown by a dog owner is another form of object play. It is, indeed, hard when watching these kinds of activities not to think that the participant is enjoying a lot of exuberant activity, the way little human kids simply run around for no particular reason, or jump up and down out of excitement. On the other hand, some object play, such as a dog playing with a stuffed animal, tossing it and tearing it apart, appears to be good practice for chasing the real thing—a training program in predation.

Object play could be useful in many regards. Perhaps juvenile object play is a form of general motor training, developing a proper use of motor and perceptual skills. And maybe it helps animals adapt to a world that needs exploring.

The third form of play is more complicated, and obviously a bit dangerous: a wide variety of mammals engage in play-fighting, and none is more fascinating and endearing than the play-fighting of young dogs, including wild canids. There's a lot of feinting, biting, throwing down, side-swiping, snapping, growling. A lot of it looks like actual aggression. It seemed quite obvious that this form of play was the canine equivalent of the ROTC, getting the young dog ready for the actual fights he or she faces in adulthood. Sometimes, though very rarely, it turns serious and one or both dogs get badly hurt.

The difficulty with these proposals is that it is hard to obtain any experimental proof that they are true. In fact, kittens who grow up without having engaged in object play have been found to be perfectly adept predators. And then there is the problem with adult animal play. If it is a training program for skills needed in later life, why would adults engage in it? Presumably they already have mastered all the skills they need. Until fairly recently, the best anyone could say about object play was that it was probably associated with predatory behavior and possibly both object play and predatory behavior were initiated by similar signals and objects. That is, there is some experimental evidence that an object that most resembled an actual prey animal was most likely to stimulate object play behavior and to hold the playful one's attention longer. In this regard, practically all of our dogs eagerly—nay, fanatically—go after squirrels in our yard (with notable lack of success), and of all the dog toys we keep in a basket in the living room, none will be destroyed faster than the stuffed squirrels.

A handful of biologists wanted to know not just what function or functions play served either immediately or later in life, but also what its *structure* was. Form follows function. It began to be clear that behavior—such as play or courtship or predation—also had form as well as function.

In the decade before Fagen wrote his landmark volume,

the University of Colorado's Marc Bekoff began filming coyotes and domestic dogs engaging in play-fighting, painstakingly studying each frame to see what exactly was going on. He found that there is a great deal more happening in play-fights than a random roughhouse. Indeed, Bekoff would go on to describe such play as a kind of dance. And among dogs, much if not most of the time the dance begins the same way, as structured as a barn dance with its dosy-dos or a tango or a waltz. It begins with one dog approaching another and performing what is now referred to technically as a play-bow. In this maneuver, the dog puts its front legs out and its chest near the ground in a kind of crouch, its head lower than its playmate's, all the while keeping its rear end high. It may bark and it usually wags its tail. From that posture, the dog can run or leap in virtually any direction as it launches the melee. Or perhaps the other dog responds to the bow by launching play. Back in the 1970s I heard this signal referred to as the *foof*, a word that evidently did not make the cut when it came to the stately vocabulary of the scientific journals—and sadly, because it is an apt and playful word for the maneuver and its meaning. It means, "hey, let's play!" and more to the point, it means "everything we do from now on is not serious, even if it gets a little rough. It's play. Foof!"

It is also, leadenly, called a play-soliciting signal. There is no poetry *there*. Foof, R.I.P.

The play-bow accomplishes more than the inauguration of happy nonhostilities. It maintains the necessary mood to keep in every participant's mind that, even though that last bite on your leg was a bit rougher than I really meant, we are still playing, right? Watch dogs playing and when things seem to be getting awfully rough, like a bite that is followed by head-shaking the

Play-bow

way a dog destroys a toy, the shaker will throw in a quick play-bow.

The play-bow, then, is a signal that seems hardwired into the dog; both wolves and coyotes use it. As far as anyone can tell, it is always understood by another dog, as if it were part of a language, not unlike a word or phrase. It is in essence an abstraction, a simple posture that has been given meaning through the course of dog evolution. What does this particular posture have to do with its meaning? Nothing more than the English word "house" or the Spanish word "casa" has to do with a building made of wood or brick or whatever. In one context, the play-bow is an agreed upon *symbol* meaning "let's play." The only other time dogs adopt this posture on a regular basis is when they wake up from a nap or from the night's sleep (dogs typically sleep sixteen hours—on and off—each day). But the stretching that leads to this posture is far more leisurely, calm. No doubt it is pleasurable. And in this context it has no meaning. Also, observations of my dogs show that in stretching the forepaws are usually close together while in the play-bow they are quite wide apart.

What if someone cheats? Say Dog A play-bows and Dog B responds. As play goes on, Dog A cheats, biting aggressively and severely hurting Dog B. Such things happen from time to time and the usual outcome is that Dog B henceforth avoids playing with Dog A. Dogs are not stupid.

Other maneuvers involved in play-fighting are also what might be called stereotyped, or ritualized. The feints, sideways leaps, the soft-mouthed ("inhibited") bites, mounting (as in sexual encounters), hip slams, falling down, racing around after one another, sudden 360-degree spin moves— these are all moves that are *sort of* but not exactly what takes place in actual fighting, just as object play is *sort of* like predatory behavior. More than likely, it is less a matter of learning the moves needed for adult fights than developing the overall motor and neurological activity needed for being a successful dog. There is, for example, some evidence that dogs who, as puppies, do not get to play have smaller (and conceivably less complex) brains.

Social play is, obviously, a highly social activity and clearly it has some down-the-road effect on the social relations of the players. Indeed, puppies who never have the chance to engage in social play are highly likely to be ill-at-ease with other dogs, if not downright aggressive toward them. But there is more to it than that, Bekoff points out.

Coyote pups, he found, are a lot more aggressive than you would expect in play. It seems that they are working out their rank in the litter, which typically means that the bigger pups win and the others lose on a consistent basis. Only after a fairly set ranking has been achieved do the coyote pups engage in the sort of play-fighting that seems to be truly playful. This pattern is not often seen among wolf pups or dog puppies, who start in social play as soon as they are physically capable. And what is remarkable in the play-fighting of dogs is that the biggest, strongest of the contestants do not always win. They often let the wimpier members prevail. They take a fall, at least momentarily. They throw the fight, or at least a few rounds. In other words, the dog that is superior handicaps itself—but to what end?

One effect of such sacrifice is, perhaps, to prolong the period of play. If Dog A is always the loser, it might grow discouraged and quit. Another possibility that Bekoff suggests is that the play-bow and the self-sacrificing may imbue in dogs a notion of fairness. This raises a Pandora's box of scientific and philosophical issues that the next chapter is devoted to. In the meantime, there is, at least at my house (and I am sure many others) a wholly different sort of social play, one that hones the difference between intense aggression and play down to a few mils (which is a unit of measurement for wire).

My backyard is separated from a neighbor's house by a large pasture and a simple wire horse fence. Every morning my neighbor lets his dogs out—two German shepherds and a Golden retriever—and they lope across the pasture to my fence. Seeing (hearing?) their approach, all of my dogs except old Amelia begin barking, yelping, racing around inside the house, causing a terrible racket until we let them out. They streak across the yard to the fence and eight dogs begin a torrent of barkage while they race back and forth on their respective sides of the fence. This goes on for as long as fifteen minutes at a time and there are usually three or four such bouts each morning, the neighbors' dogs retreating to their house across the pasture between bouts. Lips drawn back, fangs showing, the dogs snarl and bark and leap at each other. It couldn't look more aggressive, the wire fence being the only reason why it doesn't turn lethal— except for one thing. The dogs tails are wagging throughout, not just the tip of erect tails the way dogs' tails wag when they are angry. Big, wild, happy lashings back and forth. As ugly as it looks, as furious as it sounds, these dogs are, I believe, playing. I also believe that the fence itself is the "play-soliciting" object, calling forth behavior that is a lot like territorial defense. Territorial play then. The dogs look forward to each bout. It is terrific exercise. The dogs are having fun.

As noted, fun is an emotion that a lot of scientists feel uncomfortable attributing to dogs and other "lower" animals. After all, how can you be certain that a dog's mind is experiencing what we humans call fun? Often when humans are having fun they laugh. Human laughter can be many things, of course. It can be nasty laughter at someone else's expense. It can be the response to a joke. It can also be the expression of simple joy. And only humans laugh, right?

A few years back a neurobiologist, Jaak Panksepp of Bowling Green University in Ohio, was experimenting with laboratory rats and took the occasion to tickle some of them. He had already noted that when playing, the rats emitted "a cacophony" of ultrasonic (50,000Hz) chirps. And when tickled, the rats also chirped, clearly a sound of pleasure. Sonograms showed that some chirps were "more joyous" than others. The tickled rats bonded with their ticklers and sought out bouts of tickling. They were laughing, Panksepp announced, and ran into a fair amount of academic scorn. But he persisted. Tracking the part of the rat brain that lights up when the rats are playing or being tickled, he found that it was in an ancient, subcortical part, the very same place that lights up in the brain when a human laughs. Meaning that the laughter zone, and presumably laughter itself, existed long before humans or even protohumans appeared on the scene.

Looking elsewhere, Panksepp found that when a dog is playfully chasing another, they both emit short panting sounds (something like the sound if you whispered "hah" over and over). The dog being chased evidently pants more intensely than the chaser. And when dogs make this sound, the part of the brain that lights up is (no surprise) the same as that of the laughing rats and humans.

Since hearing about this, I have attentively listened to my own dogs for signs of laughter. I have noticed that when one or the other of them comes up to greet me, it often sounds like it is whispering "hah" over and over again, this coupled with a lowered head, the sides of the mouth drawn back in what appears to be a smile, and the tail vigorously, one might even say joyously wagging.

"Gentle Darwin," Panksepp has written, "was prescient when he coaxed us to see our own emotional nature as continuous with that of our fellow animals." The neurobiologist went on to say, "Although some still regard laughter as a uniquely human trait, honed in the Pleistocene, the joke's on them."

JUNO AND AMELIA ("IT'S MINE! MINE!")

## Chapter Eleven

# The Mind of Dogs

D o dogs have the brains to think?

This question and variants of it, asked over a great deal of time probably beginning some fourteen or so thousand years ago, are still the cause of fascinating philosophical and scientific disputation. Some of this is a result of the amour propre of the human animal. Many scholars define those traits that are considered part of the human bag of tricks so finely that only humans possess anything like them. This keeps the human ego in a state of proper health, one supposes. Cultural anthropologists, for example, have defined what they call—in hushed tones—Culture (roughly, everything which is passed on nonbiologically) so narrowly that even if young chimpanzees learn to make simple tools by imitating the example of adults, it cannot be Culture. If, on the other hand, a twelve-year-old boy imitates his uncle and successfully changes the oil of a car, this is Culture. To be sure, a simple stick to fish termites out of a mound is not as sophisticated as an internal combustion engine, but often a draconian line is drawn across what would otherwise appear to some as a continuum.

Consciousness is another feature of the human animal which one risks one's neck attributing to "lower" animals like our closest relatives chimpanzees or, God forbid, dogs (75 percent of whose genetic code is indistinguishable from ours). Most philosophers, psychologists, and others engaged in the study of the mind deny consciousness to dogs. By consciousness, they do not speak of being awake or out cold but of a higher understanding of oneself as a self with a past, present, and future and various other complex sorts of awareness. Of course, dogs and chimps and others do not do astronomy and consider their place in universe, or ponder the meaning of life in the context of inevitable death. Still, denying such creatures *any* form of consciousness strikes me as a bit presumptuous since philosophers and psychologists are yet to come up even with a definition of consciousness to which they can all subscribe. How can you confidently deny to some creature that which you don't yet understand well enough to define, you ask? It happens all the time.

Admittedly, scientists are hard put to find ways to say with utter certainty that dogs have such mental capacities as self-awareness, or the knowledge that other dogs have minds that work something like theirs, and act accordingly. This latter feature, by the way, is called Theory of Mind: which is to say that you believe that I possess a mind not wholly dissimilar from yours, so you can imagine that what I am thinking is not wholly different than what you may be thinking. It is easier to imagine that a dog's mind is purely and only reactive, dealing with events as they are perceived and in a largely programmed manner based on genes and a wee bit of experience, especially experience in the formative years of puppydom.

But Charles Darwin and many after him have been willing to point to a continuum of animals and people occurring in evolution, that produced varying levels of such things as memory, intelligence, self-awareness, and so forth, leading to varying degrees of reasoning capacity and consciousness. There is no doubt in anyone's mind that human beings have taken such attributes to the current extreme of power and intensity (though we surely have a ways to go as a species in the reasoning department). On the other hand, all mammalian brains including ours operate largely on the same principles with much the same equipment. They all have nerve cells (neurons made of the same stuff and in the same way), and hormones that stimulate the brain and such organs as the pituitary and thyroid glands.

Each neuron consists of a cell body with thousands of receptor sites, meaning that each neuron can send out thousands of messages simultaneously, and the dog's brain contains billions of neurons—less than ours to be sure, but even a single billion individual anythings crammed into a blob the size of a navel orange is really unimaginable, ungraspable even by our human brain's fifteen billion neurons in concert. And most of the dog's neurons do much the same thing as ours, using up to thirty different substances to help messages cross from one neuron to another—a place of continuous actions of indescribable complexity.

Like ours, for example, the dog brain has two centers given over to sleep (and one to wakefulness). The sleep center in the back of the brain is responsible for deep sleep, the other in front is for light sleep. The deep sleep of a dog is hard to distinguish from the deep sleep of humans, called REM sleep for the rapid eye movement that occurs. And this, in both humans and dogs, is the time when one dreams. How many times have I seen one or the other of our sleeping dogs engaged in a chase, emitting happy little yelps, feet churning, sometimes going on for several minutes. As veterinarian Bruce Fogle has pointed out, if the dog's wake center malfunctions, the dog may suddenly lapse into deep sleep; if it happens often enough, it is called narcolepsy, a condition to which some humans are also given, including a former Secretary of the Smithsonian Institution. Among dogs it occurs only among Dobermans, poodles, dachshunds and Labrador retrievers.

It's as easy to go overboard with the similarities in brain structure and substance as it is to downplay them. There are still people who think dogs are automatons in fur. There are also plenty of people who think dogs are little people in fur. Perched somewhere in between is the truth which, simply stated, is that dogs are dogs. It is useful to remember that whatever they possess of intelligence, memory, emotions and all that—regardless of how similar or different they may be from ours—has come about, just like their brains, in response to the necessities of a dog's life.

Like humans, dogs have a part of the brain called the cerebral cortex. This is the wrinkly sheath that overlies the rest of the brain and is, to put it oversimply, in charge of making sense of all the various inputs to the brain from the senses. The dog's cerebral cortex is smaller and less complex than that of a human, but the greatest difference occurs in the frontal lobes of the cerebral cortex. These are the areas involved in human intellectual functions, the great organizer of data that Temple Grandin suggests doesn't work perfectly in autistic humans, leaving them with a lot of raw—and to some degree unanalyzable—data. Dogs have frontal lobes, but they are much smaller relative to the overall brain than those of humans and would appear to be unable to put all of their raw data together. (In the same way, the olfactory bulbs in the back of the brain are tremendous in dogs, puny in humans.) But the frontal lobes of dogs is where their temperament or personality lies, and what makes them alert and interested—when they are—and is thought to be the seat of their intelligence. Recalling the rule that form and function are linked, one needs to confess that a dog's pituitary probably serves much the same function as yours, and its smaller frontal lobes some doggish version of what yours do.

All of this seems fairly abstract, doesn't it? Temperament, personality, intelligence, thinking—these are all pretty vague labels for certain attributes, skills, talents, and activities, few of which have universally agreed-upon definitions for humans, much less dogs. So what can dogs actually *do* mentally? Are there ways to peer into the intellect of a dog to see if it is self-aware, capable of planning ahead, learning by imitation—all those acts that fall under the rubric of cognition? Are they truly conscious? Believe me, this is a copse full of thorns red with the blood of innumerable researchers but we will soldier on into this territory and possibly, with enough hip-swiveling, we can slip past many of the thorns. (That is three metaphors in one sentence for those of you who count such things.)

First of all, do dogs have memory? Of course. For one thing, without a memory they couldn't learn anything or recognize you. When Curry, our Navajo dog, came to live with us, he got caught in a doorway where the door closed on him, and ever since he is extremely wary of entering the house, needing reassurance that the way is clear, a regrettable bit of learning memorialized in his brain for more than a decade. I believe that dogs, like horses, have an unfailing memory of bad things that have happened to them.

Do dogs have personalities? To anyone who has owned a few dogs, this seems to be a stupid question. But on the other hand, scientists would like to pin it down with the kind of certainty and accuracy that is associated with numbers. In the first place: what are the parameters of dog personality, and how do you test for them? Samuel Gosling of the University of Texas at Austin and several collaborators set out to assess the personalities of various dogs and the personalities of their owners according to a model that is widely in use in psychology departments for determining human personalities. The subjects in this study were ranked for four personality traits: *affection* (something like human agreeableness), *energy* (something like human extraversion), *reactivity* (analogous to human neuroticism) and *intelligence* (analogous to human openness and intellect).

The point of the study was to see if accepted ways of rating human personalities could be applied with the same coherence and consensus to dogs. The dogs were rated by their owners, by someone else who knew the dogs, and then by strangers rating photographs of the dogs in action. It turned out that everyone pretty much agreed, dog by dog, on their particular personality traits, as well as the traits of the humans involved. So the door is open for all sorts of personality studies, making it possible perhaps to link such things as ecological factors and evolutionary histories to individual dog personalities

Of course, almost everyone with a pure-bred dog will expound on that breed's built-in personality, and one would expect that different breeds would show different personalities or at least different approaches to their worlds. And by way of helping people choose what breed of dog would be suitable for different lifestyles (and human personalities) and other circumstances such as environment (as in city apartments versus open meadows), Benjamin L. Hart, a veterinarian, and his wife Lynette, both of the University of California at Davis, set out to make essentially numerical measures of thirteen key dog traits, and how these traits appear in different breeds. They laid this all out in a highly accessible popular book, *The Perfect Puppy* (which is listed in the bibliography). It is not the purpose of this book to go into detail on all of this, but it is important to know how they arrived at some of this material. They asked the opinions of numerous vets, trainers, and other dog people, and tried to assess what the predictive value of the thirteen traits is in any given breed. Overall, they found that such traits as excitability—how intensely a dog reacts to the arrival of the FedEx truck or other such stimuli—has a very high predictive value. In other words, if a given breed shows up as highly excitable, you can pretty well count on that. Excessive barking, on the other hand, is only of moderate predictive value, meaning that you could easily choose a dog from a particular breed that is supposed to be likely to bark to excess and find to your relief that your dog doesn't do that. Sadly, ease of housebreaking—one of the most desirable of all dog traits—has a very low predictive value.

The Harts' book goes on to profile fifty-six breeds using easy-to-read bar charts. For example, the Australian shepherd has very low excitability, high general activity, low snapping at children, and low excessive barking. It is highly trainable and playful, moderately destructive, and demands a lot of affection. It is moderate on territorial barking and low on aggression toward other dogs.

Contrast this with the West Highland white terrier, a little dog. It is highly excitable, hyperactive, snaps at children a lot, barks excessively, does a lot of watchdog barking, is aggressive to other dogs, and tries hard to dominate its owner. It's very destructive and quite playful. The only trait in which it ranks especially low is obedience training.

The Harts' scheme is so far the best way to apply the phrase "each to his own taste" to the selection of a dog breed. Nevertheless, what you see in an actual litter is extremely unpredictable. What looks like the friendliest of the puppies may turn out to be a biter. The biggest puppy may become a wimp. A great deal of the personality of a dog can come from what is learned, not so much its genes and its breed. The most predictive trait, some say—the trait that if present in the puppy will almost certainly continue in the adult—is fear. And fear in a dog can lead to very bad things indeed.

Another caveat that many dog experts assert is that there is more variation in behavior among the members of a given breed than there are between any two breeds.

Do dogs learn by observation and imitation? Some people think not but such a denial is unsustainable in the face of daily life. Our Cattle Dog Ding, for example, unfortunately needed only a few observations of me opening a screen door to realize that he could rise up on his back legs and with his forepaws push the door handle, opening the door and escaping. We took to closing the wooden front door as well as the screen door and it did not take long for Ding to pull the handle on the wooden door down and toward him with his left front paw and slip his right paw into the resulting crack. Examples abound of dogs learning by observation and imitation—perhaps most notably the way young herd dogs or sled dogs learn from their elders how to go about their appointed tasks.

How else do they learn? Pavlov's dog is the most famous canine student. (Actually there were several, but it has been reduced to one in the vernacular.) Simply described: Pavlov, a great student of saliva for which he received the Nobel Prize, rang a bell when producing the smell of meat for the dog. Upon smelling meat, the dog salivated as dogs do, and learned to associate the sound of the bell with the appearance of the meat smell. Before long, all it took for the dog to salivate was the sound of the bell. This is called classic conditioning (where the word conditioning is simply academic patois for learning). The bell set off an unconscious, automatic, emotional reaction. It seems that negative classic conditioning—where fear or pain is involved—takes less time, as was the case with Ding and the door.

Operant conditioning, on the other hand, is a more active learning mode—indeed one might say more conscious. This is where the dog or other subject learns to get a reward by pushing the right lever with its nose. The idea is that any behavior that is regularly rewarded will soon increase, and the opposite—what goes unrewarded may become less. Most good dog trainers learn how to use positive operant conditioning to teach dogs a host of obedience and other skills. The difficulty is that the trainer (maybe you) has to provide the reward almost instantaneously, within up to fifteen or so seconds, for the dog to make the association between the behavior and the reward. Trainers or owners who use punishments (mild punishment, one hopes, such as saying "BAAAAD dog!" or spraying the malefactor with lemon water or bitter apple if they bark too much) need to inflict the punishment in a similar amount of time—fifteen seconds—or the dog will simply be bewildered, unable to connect its act to that of the trainer. All of which, of course, will produce an increment of ill will between the two.

How far can operant conditioning take a dog in terms of memory and what can be thought of as thinking—or cognition? One startling answer arose in 2004 in the vocabulary of a nine-year old German border collie, a family pet named Rico. In the first place, Rico's family reported to the Max Planck Institute for Evolutionary Anthropology, that Rico's vocabulary stood at about 200. Scientists at the institute then found that unlike most dogs, Rico could learn to associate a name and an object after just one exposure to the combination. Psychologists call this fast mapping, and it was thought that the only creatures capable of it were human toddlers. They tested him by having some forty of his toys in an adjacent room, into which he went after his owner told him to fetch one or two of them. Rico was right thirty-seven times out of forty tries. Then the scientists repeated the tests, but each put a new toy in the room in addition to other familiar toys. The owner called out a new word and on seven times out of ten tries, Rico picked up the unfamiliar toy.

Evidently Rico was able to appreciate the fact that a new word referred to an object that did not already have a name. This ability clearly suggests a kind of protosequential thinking at least. "That's a new sound. All these have sounds for them. This one doesn't. Aha!" This is equivalent to how three-year-old human children learn their way around the language, and it is has not been seen in apes, dolphins, or parrots who have nevertheless shown a great capacity to learn what human words refer to. (Perhaps no one has thought to test them on this.) "Of course," Julia Fischer, one of the biologists participating in the study, told the *Washington Post*, "for a child, a word very rapidly means more than it does for a dog. They will quickly know it's a color word or an activity word." Yet for doing this particular task, Rico is as smart as a three-year-old child.

Most scholars in this realm have assumed that only humans had the perceptual and cognitive mechanism that underlie the development of language. "What this shows," said Marc Bekoff of the University of Colorado, "is that other animals possess those perceptual abilities."

Is Rico the exception, a kind of idiot savant among dogs, or are most dogs capable of such feats? At least one other scientist has reported similar capability on the part of two dogs, and more studies will surely ensue. It remains to be seen.

From time to time the question of canine intelligence arises. Are some breeds more intelligent than others? Probably, but it is extremely difficult to say since measuring intelligence among humans is not something anyone really agrees upon, never mind dogs.

Various people have attempted to rank dog intelligence by breed—one of these is Stanley Coren, the psychologist whose preface adorns this book. He made an extensive list of breeds by intelligence with Afghans at the low end of the totem pole and border collies near the top, the appropriateness of part of which is born out by Rico. But Ray Coppinger, the Hampshire College biologist, takes exception to such a list, pointing out that dog breeds are, among other things, bred for specific purposes and their intelligence presumably is appropriate to these purposes. So such rankings, he says, are essentially meaningless. On the other hand, trainability is an aspect of intelligence that is of special interest to the dog owner, and also is easier to measure. Coren has since produced a list of breeds ranked by trainability. Interestingly, the border collie stands at the top of the list and the Afghan at the bottom. In general, retrievers, poodles, and herding and working dogs all seem to be high in trainability while hounds and terriers are the lowest. Coren's trainability list is one of this book's appendixes.

Finally, in such matters as trainability and intelligence (whatever that really means), most dog people agree that—as we have said before—there is as much, if not more, individual variability within breeds as there are differences among breeds. And of course, in the world of crossbreeds—aka mutts—there is usually hardly any way of predicting. Mutts do tend to avoid some of the high-strung traits that so often characterize purebreds.

Moving on from the vagaries of intelligence, where do dogs stand in the realm of self-awareness, empathy, and consciousness? For some people, all of these characteristics are simply denied to any creature but *Homo sapiens*. For yet others, apes and some monkeys are allowed a toe or two over the threshold. For example, it has been shown to the satisfaction of many students of animal cognition that a chimpanzee has a sense of self, that it exists as a being separate from other chimpanzees. The tip-off has to do with mirrors. If you set a chimp in front of a mirror, it will often begin to make faces at the reflection. Next time, adorn the chimp's face with a bit of lipstick and then put it in front of the mirror. Before long it will begin to touch the places on its face where the lipstick is, not on where it shows up on the image in the mirror. The chimp, then, realizes that the mirror shows a reflection (or some kind of version) of the chimp itself. The chimp is self-aware. (The test is not perfect, it seems. Some chimps do not respond as expected.) Dogs, on the other hand, will typically walk past a mirror, paying no heed whatsoever to the flat image on the glass. Not only do they not see the image as themselves, but they don't really see it as a dog. This was taken as prima facie evidence that dogs are not self-aware.

Marc Bekoff chose to disagree. Nonalpha dogs rarely stare straight at another dog. And perhaps more telling, apes have binocular vision, and vision is their most important sense in that they derive the most information about their world from looking at it. Dogs, he points out, rely mostly on smell and the reflection of a dog in a mirror gives off no smell.

Bekoff is one of those few people who can just about put himself into a dog's mind, and his neighbors in the hills above Boulder probably knew him well enough to know that he had not totally lost his mind when he began racing ahead of his dog—a German shepherd–Rottweiler mix called Jethro—in the snow, carefully lifting up the snow his dog and others peed on and moving it to other locations. This was, in fact, science in action.

Bekoff timed Jethro's arrival at a given patch of yellow snow—did he arrive ten seconds after it had been placed, or from ten second to two minutes, or from two to five minutes. He carefully watched Jethro's behavior at each patch of yellow snow, noting, of course, whether it was Jethro's urine, or that of other males, or females. In each time interval there were slight differences in behavior—whether Jethro sniffed a long time or not, or spent a long time or short time or no time covering the urine with his own. Overall, Jethro clearly recognized his own urine, distinguishing it from that of other dogs by significantly different behavior. Which is to say, Jethro was aware of himself as different from the other dogs. Bekoff says that dogs have a sense of "body-ness"—ownership of body parts like paws—and a sense of "mine-ness," as in territory or bones. Do they experience what might be called "I-ness?" That is harder to say, harder to prove.

In the chapter on play, we saw that dogs will reverse their roles from dominance to submission to dominance and so forth—in other words, winning and losing. This way the smaller, or less athletic, or more submissive dog gets to win a few which is almost certainly rewarding. The dogs thus learn an elementary kind of fairness, and this suggests that a dog has a sense not only of itself but of its playmate as an individual. Could this be a sign that dogs have empathy for one another? It has been shown experimentally that rats have empathy for each other if they are cagemates. Rats who saw their cagemates in pain were more sensitive to pain than those who were tested alone. There is, thus, a social component to the experience of pain. The researcher, Jeffrey Mogil of McGill University, spoke of an "emotional contagion" between the animals.

Presumably dogs are similar in this regard. When one of my dogs yelps because something hurt it, all the others who are present run up to it and sniff its rear end and its face. Are they concerned for the hurt dog, and trying to see how seriously it hurts, or is this some kind of doggish version of "there but for the grace of God go I?"

A relatively new discovery in neuroscience may explain this kind of behavior—what we might call empathy. In at least four different parts of the human brain, what are called "mirror neurons" fire when the owner of that brain sees someone who is sad, or angry, or kicking a football, or eating ice cream, or any other expression or activity. And if the someone is, let us say sad, her lower lip trembling and so forth, the other person experiences the same sensation of sadness. If I reach for a glass, certain neurons fire in my brain: if you pick up a glass, the same neurons in my brain fire. In other words, in my brain I *simulate* your actions and can pretty well know what your intentions are. It is a kind of neurological imitation, and was first discovered in monkeys, and later in humans where mirror neurons are many and highly complex. Experts peg the human mirror neurons' complexity to the complexity of human society and human abilities to imitate, and we know that dogs have at least a limited capacity for imitation. Indeed, experts say that other animals—monkeys, apes, and possibly dolphins, elephants, and dogs—probably have at least rudimentary mirror neurons. These remarkable brain cells put a whole new light on a great many human endeavors from psychiatry to training athletes. And if they are indeed found to be present in other highly social animals, it will put an unarguable biological basis for such things as empathy and possibly other prerequisites for consciousness existing in highly social nonhuman animals, including dogs and wolves.

So far we have tracked the likelihood of a sense of fairness among dogs engaged in social play, and it seems unlikely that any form of fairness could come about without some kind of personal concern for others—that is, a kind of empathy which dogs almost certainly acquire early on in their lives, whether by mirror neurons or by smell or by a combination of senses and neuronal processes. They appear to a have a sense of themselves. My wife Susanne points out that a dog can get a little concerned if you take off its old, grubby collar and provide it with a new one. This may be simply canine aversion to change, but it could also be that the new collar—by appearance or smell or both—just doesn't seem to the dog to be "me" yet.

The next step is to inquire if dogs are self-conscious. Human consciousness—in most attempted definitions—includes the capacity to reflect upon the thinking process by which one is reflecting on something. This may well be beyond a dog's mental capacities. But Marc Bekoff, in 2006, held out hope that neurobiological studies will be able to show that dogs, among other social animals, have similar neural reactions as humans do when humans reflect upon their own thought processes. Or not.

He proposes that self-cognizance should be "most developed in long-lived, group-living animals in which individuals have repeated interactions that are both cooperative and competitive, with the same suite" of group members (or what scientists call conspecifics). These are animal societies in which mated pairs and other group members interact throughout their lives, and practice variations on "nepotism, reciprocity, competition and selfishness." Such animals would benefit from revising their own behavior in light of how their conspecifics have reacted to them. If Darwin's suggestion that such mental capacities lie along a continuum, one could fruitfully look into a lot of other social animals besides dogs and wolves. Bekoff suggests research on honeybees, lions, meerkats, gray parrots, and acorn woodpeckers, among others, believing that comparative studies between species can pay off in spades.

So if the question is are dogs self-conscious, the answer is that we don't know yet, but a firmer notion may not be too far off. Part of the answer will hinge not just on neuronal firings in experimental situations, but also determining if dogs have the Theory of Mind we mentioned earlier. This refers to the theory (or lack of it) that each individual has about other creatures and their minds. Does that group member have a mind that is enough like mine that it can read my signals and act accordingly? The evidence seems to say that dogs do indeed have a theory of mind. The use of the play-bow as a signal to say "let's play," and to say, later on when a player gets a bit too rough, "oops, sorry, we're still playing, right?" would suggest that even puppies have a sense that their littermates all think pretty much alike. In humans, such a theory of mind doesn't come about until about the age of four. Stanley Coren suggests a simple test that anyone with a dog who will fetch can try. Throw a ball several times for the dog to retrieve, then turn your back. The dog, realizing that you won't throw the ball if it is not visible to you, will run around and place the ball in front of you. So Coren concludes on this topic, "if we credit two- to four-year-old humans with consciousness and reasoning, then, in the absence of data to the contrary, it seems appropriate that we grant the same to dog."

Reasoning? Wait a minute. Do dogs use reason or something very like it to solve problems? There is a great deal of anecdotal evidence to suggest that they do from time to time. One of our dogs behaved in such a way, even when she was a puppy, to make us think that she could apply a kind of planning and deception in order to achieve a goal. This was Teacup, the dog from the Hopi Reservation, part German shepherd and heaven knows what else but probably a bit of coyote somewhere back there.

When we got her, we decided to be like true grown-up dog owners and put her in a crate at night or when we were leaving the house for an errand. And Teacup took happily to her crate, trotting into the bedroom with us at our bedtime, which was typically at nine o'clock, and bouncing into her crate. The crate had several wire mesh windows from which she would watch us get into bed.

At that time in our lives, the Navajo Rez dog, Curry, would get on the bed and sleep there, it being the only place where he felt safe enough to be handled, even by us. It turns out that Teacup also observed Curry getting on the bed. About three weeks of this passed and then one night, at about ten of nine, Teacup left us in the living room and went to the bedroom. At nine we retired, but did not see Teacup in the bedroom. Finally we spotted her, lying in the narrow place between the bed and a wall, with her head under the dust ruffle. She didn't move and we wondered what was up. We decided to get in bed, shut off the light, and see what happened. About five minutes later, Teacup jumped up on the bed and went to sleep.

The next night the same events occurred except this time all that stuck out from the dust ruffle was her tail. Could she have thought out these moves in advance? We don't know. It's what scientists call an anecdote, meaning insufficient evidence. Anyway, we got rid of the crate. We have a big bed.

A lot of people are less interested in their dogs' reasoning abilities than they are in whether their dogs love them. Dogs certainly can look and act like they love you—limpid eyes, the joy with which they greet you, their obvious contentedness when snoozing at your feet, all that. Cynics exist who say that all of this is a sham, as is a lot of other dog behavior. Dogs, the cynics say, have clearly been naturally and artificially selected over the millennia to act as if they really experience love for us when they are merely "designed" to make us believe they love us. It's an act put on to insure that we keep on rubbing their tummies and feeding them. This school of thought points out that chimps, our closest genetic relatives in the animal kingdom, do not by any measure fall in love. They don't spend much time courting or mating or remaining with the partners they have mated with.

On the other hand, such things as romantic love probably didn't suddenly show up when modern humans evolved from our hominid forebears. If it has no evolutionary history, it probably doesn't exist at all. As Marc Bekoff points out, most mammals and even birds share the brain systems and chemistry that are the basis for human love. Levels of the neurotransmitter called dopamine go way up when humans fall in full-bore, lusting, dreamy, breathtaking love, and so does dopamine in rats when looking forward to a sexual encounter. Oxytocin, a hormone that is common to all mammals, is also involved in courtship and love in humans. Why not dogs? Of course, it is true that, like chimps, dogs don't do much lingering with their mates the way wolves and other canids do. But many of them do spend a lot of what is clearly affectionate time with their human owners. Impugning such apparent displays of affection by dogs as a full-time con job seems like a rather large stretch. Con artists have to work very hard lest the mark see through it all. The simpler explanation: that at least some dogs experience an attachment to a human or several humans that looks like a kind of love and probably is just that—a doggish version of love. The differences in many such emotions between dogs and humans are, I am convinced, a matter of degree, not kind.

You want to argue about it?

Foof.

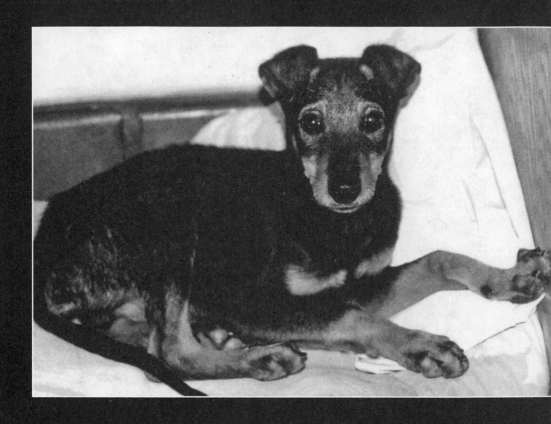

CURRY AT FOUR MONTHS

# Some Thoughts on Training

As noted earlier, this is not a book about training dogs, and I have also confessed earlier on in this book that we have not paid much attention to training our six dogs. We wanted a certain level of obedience (come when called) and, of course, house-breaking. But we simply didn't see ourselves adopting a training regime that called for daily lessons, or even weekly lessons. The dogs get good exercise running the fences and on the occasional walk. But once we had both Teacup the Hopi dog, and Juno the Australian mix, both about six months old, we were tempted into taking the two of them to an obedience class.

The obedience class took place in a large room in which some fifteen people and their dogs stood in a big circle while a most demonstrative woman explained her system, which included a training collar cleverly made of lots of separate pieces of thick wire connected in such a way that if you pulled on the leash, the wires all poked the dog's neck. Teacup and Juno didn't seem to mind this very much, and we continued in the class for two sessions, the net result being that when we said "By me!" the dogs adopted the position known most commonly as Heel, standing next to our left side, or walking there without tugging on the leash, and then doing both without the leash.

At the end of the second session, the demonstrative women explained that the following week, we would do something else: we would teach the dog to lie on its side and to be still and uncomplaining when we put our foot on its neck. This was, I gathered, necessary for the dogs to know who was boss.

Susanne and I took the two dogs home and looked at each other. No way. We didn't need to discuss it. We knew we were not going to do that.

The dogs already knew that we were the boss. They had learned to heel (though with a different phrase) when we told them to. I could not imagine a scenario in which it would be necessary to pin Teacup to the ground by standing on her neck. What useful thing would she learn from that? It struck me as a merely arbitrary show of force, a kind of bullying. There are, I think, laws about bosses who bully the staff and, deep down, bullies are typically a bit insecure.

I remembered reading in some dog training book (there must be several thousand dog training books) that you should never let your dog's head be above yours, otherwise it will get the idea that it is the dominant one. Well, I thought to myself, what if I am lying in the yard in the sun and a dog walks up to be with me? Or what if I am lying on the sofa and little Jupiter jumps up and falls asleep on my chest, as he has done since he was a puppy? Have I lost my place on the totem pole?

Ridiculous.

If I have learned anything in the course of writing this book, it is that it is almost certainly a bad idea to do negative, punitive training of dogs except perhaps in certain special cases, though I am not sure what those cases would be. A friend of mine got himself a pair of Anatolian shepherds and realized pretty quickly that he needed to get some heavy-duty training going on, because they were big, rough, and potentially dangerous even as six-month olds. No one but the immediate family could enter the house safely if they were loose inside. He took them to a trainer who offered to break them in English or in German. And right off the bat the trainer proceeded to yank them on their chain leashes, literally throwing them through the air to crash on the ground. Other stunts followed in the ensuing days that would show these dogs who was the * * * * * boss. After a couple of weeks of this, the trainer pronounced the two dogs trained. My friend sent one of them to live on a huge ranch, and took the other home, but it was so intimidated and given to violence (fear bites) that, heartbroken, he had to have it put down.

This is an extreme case, of course, and it would be very surprising if this particular trainer has much of a success rate at turning out calm and safe family pets. But many less violent dog trainers are hung up on the role of dominance, the pecking order, the alpha dog. The principal requirement of the celebrated Cesar Millan, the Dog Whisperer of National Geographic television fame, is that a dog owner has to establish firmly that the owner, not the dog, is dominant, and to remind the dog of this regularly. And this is necessary because dogs are derived from wolves, and wolf packs are highly stratified, with an alpha pair dominating the life of the pack. But as noted earlier, most of this kind of behavior—the supposed daily dominance wars—does not take place in the wild. Most of this kind of behavior among wolves has been observed in captive wolf groups where the members of the "pack" were unrelated. In the wild, wolf packs consist typically of a bunch of relatives, usually including an alpha (older) pair and their offspring. There is no question in such circumstances about who is the boss, and careful observation of wolves in the wild by David Mech and others suggests that wolf behavior within a pack is based as much, if not more, on cooperation as on dominance.

Millan is, in fact, a punitive dog trainer, using choke collars, treadmills, and other techniques to browbeat a dog (usually a problem dog) into a subservient fealty to the pack leader (him, and by extension, the dog's owner). Mark Derr recently pointed out in the *New York Times*, "that almost from birth, they [dogs] are attentive to people, and that most are eager to please, given proper instruction and encouragement." In the past forty or so years, great strides have been made in understanding the development and behavior of dogs. Along with this understanding has come the realization that dogs (like people) learn more, and more thoroughly, when they are treated as individuals, with patience and rewards. Most modern dog trainers understand this.

And when, for whatever reason, something in the relationship of the dog and its owner, or two dogs in a household goes wrong, it is time to call in a professional trainer. Finding trainers who base their work more on the notion of cooperation rather than on dominance may be hard to find in a given neighborhood, but it is worth the search.

*Appendix A*

# Dog Bites

If few things are more endearing than puppies playing, few of us who are not police officers or soldiers will ever run into something more terrifying than a large dog in attack mode. And almost five million people a year in the United States experience that kind of fright—from being bitten by a dog. In all, 800,000 dog bites require medical attention each year, and nearly half of those send the afflicted into the emergency room, according to Kenneth Morgan Phillips, who operates the Web site www.dogbitelaw.com and is a Los Angeles lawyer whose practice is solely in behalf of dogs, dog owners, and dog-bite victims. In fact, Phillips reports, dog bites are second only to baseball accidents in sending people to the ER. On average, some 2,800 letter carriers are bitten each year, typically on their legs. The most frequently bitten people are children, and they are typically bitten on the face by a dog that belongs to their family or to a friend's family. Male dogs, particularly unneutered ones, are more likely to bite than females.

An estimated seventy million dogs live in the United States. Between 1991 and 1998, the canine population grew only 2 percent, but the number of medically treated bites rose from 1986 to 1994 by 35 percent. Public health workers consider this a "silent epidemic," and the Centers for Disease Control and Prevention estimates that the medical costs were more than $164 million in 2002, while the insurance industry pegs the annual insurance costs for dog bites at $2 billion. All of these estimates are probably low. Many dog bites go unrecorded.

What explains all this? The dog industry is wont to say that there are no bad dogs, no bad breeds, just bad owners. Like many bumper-sticker oversimplifications, there is a fair amount of truth to this. Lots of dog owners have no idea whatsoever of what their responsibilities are to the dog and to the public. Any dog who is left alone chained up outside, or otherwise mistreated, can get frustrated, frantic, and turn on people or other dogs if given the chance. Bad owners do make bad dogs.

Others look at the breeds most often reported in cases of severe dog attacks, including lethal attacks, and conclude that certain breeds should be banned or at least restricted. Among the breeds that are extremely hard to insure in the United States are pit bulls, Rottweilers—the two breeds that are responsible these days for about three-fourths of the annual average of twenty-five or so lethal dog attacks in the United States—along with Akitas, Bernese Mountain dogs, Presa Canarios, Chow chows, Dobermans, Huskies (except Siberian huskies), Rhodesian Ridgebacks and some others. Actuarial logic is hard to argue with. Even the president of People for the Ethical Treatment of Animals, the fairly radical animal rights group, has written that pit bulls should be banned everywhere.

Opponents of such bans say that to do so is akin to racism, that owners of a gentle dog from a so-called dangerous breed should not be penalized, that countries like Great Britain and the Netherlands instituted total bans on pit bulls, for example, and found after several years that incidents of dog bites did not diminish. Other breeds must have taken up the slack, so to speak, and ban opponents say that if you ban, say, pit bulls, another breed will soon surface as the attack dog of choice. Attack dog?

A sociological finding is that your neighborhood crack dealer is not likely to be seen on the streets walking a pair of Corgis. Street tough guys want threatening dogs. And people who engage in the illegal sport of dogfights do not arrange such bouts between Yorkshire terriers. Pit bulls and some other breeds were originally bred for fighting and some—who knows how many?—who are picked up in cities and taken to the pound were brutalized to make them vicious and then simply abandoned when they were less able to win fights. Pit bulls, by the way, are of several kinds, less a single breed than a category of dog like retrievers or hounds. Most pit bulls have broad heads, big deep chests and spectacularly strong jaws. They can weigh from twenty to a hundred pounds. Some people distinguish between American Staffordshire terriers, English Staffordshire terriers and plain pit bulls. There is some evidence that most or some of the English ones have been bred for gentleness over some fifty generations and are less likely to be aggressive than the others. Many pit bulls (and other dogs from hard-to-insure breeds) are sweet and loving pets. There simply is a great deal of factual and ethical and even legal murk in all these discussions. But it is wiser in the long run to say that genes, early development, and owners all have a great effect on dogs.

Lawmakers have an extremely difficult time with all this, the problems beginning with how to define a dangerous dog. One that has bitten someone once? Twice? One that bites other dogs? One that terrorizes a neighborhood in some other way? Different jurisdictions have different definitions.

Then, what is society to do with a dog deemed a threat? Put it down? Demand the owner and the dog go to some sort of rehab training? Make the owner responsible to keep the dog leashed and out of the way? Muzzled? Does a city or town have the right to restrict peoples' dogs by breed? Some say no. Others point to the laws based on public health considerations that restrict people from owning goats or cows or chickens in cities. Why not restrict the freedoms of dogs given to biting people? What about hybrids—mutts, that is? Are there particular crossbreeds that also should be restricted in some manner? Should people be encouraged to obtain mutts which may be more likely to be free of some of the flaws—such as excess excitability—that can and often do result from excessive inbreeding to maintain the purity (and plenitude) of a given breed? Mutts have a lot going for them if you find the right one or ones.

Speaking of crossbreeds: I can hear the howls of protest, but it seems obvious to me that wolf-dog crosses are simply a terrible idea. Dogs, in the process of domestication, traveled a long way physiologically and psychologically from wolves, even though their genes are not so easily distinguished. Putting wolves back into dogs is in no way likely to improve the dog. For example, as biologist Ray Coppinger points out, good sled dogs are the product of a great deal of careful breeding directed at making them good at pulling sleds. To cross a good sled dog with a wolf would simply diminish the sled dog's acquired skills—physical and psychological skills that wolves do not possess. Not only that, but at some point in the early life of a wolf-dog cross, the adult, un-neotenized wolf psychology is likely to reassert itself, leaving the animal with a bewildering array of opposite urges that produce an extremely high risk of violence. Ninety percent of wolf-dog crosses are put to sleep by the age of two. What to do with those wolf-dog crosses who are now in the hands of owners? Neuter them, certainly, and make it illegal to deliberately hybridize domestic and wild canids.

While there is no question that the world is full of bad (meaning irresponsible) dog owners, and that the various periods of development from puppy to adult are extremely important, as is exercise, good nutrition, and training where needed, it makes no sense to completely ignore the genetic makeup of individual breeds (or, for that matter, what you can tell about a crossbreed's genetic heritage). A lot of big guard dogs like the Anatolian shepherd were in old times left alone for long periods, fending for themselves, guarding flocks of sheep in the mountains, and protecting them from predators like lions which they were perfectly capable of killing. For the owners of sheep and other livestock, such dogs were in a sense professional partners, highly valued for their work. Some of these dogs are still used for that purpose in the United States, while others are kept as pets. They are fiercely loyal to their human family and many retain a considerable suspicion of anyone—human or nonhuman—whom they perceive as a stranger and possible predator. Common sense would suggest that one of these dogs—or any huge guard dog breed, for that matter—could prove to be a little hard to handle. It takes careful breeding over many generations (say, forty like the silver foxes?) to make a big change in a breed's overall psychology.

What to do about this silent epidemic of dog bites? Community-based programs seem to work best. They include educating dog owners and prospective dog owners about, among many other things, teaching their children how to behave around a dog, mandatory insurance for certain dangerous breeds and known dangerous dogs—and maybe all dogs over fifty pounds—making it clear that owners are liable for injuries brought about by their dogs, restricting certain breeds (such as making it mandatory that they be muzzled in public, making it illegal for convicted felons to own certain breeds), restricting the number of dogs from such breeds in a family. People who engage in dog-fighting contests and other forms of inhumane treatment should, of course, be hammered.

In most places, dog licenses are mandatory, and part of that process is producing evidence that the dog has received immunizing shots against rabies and several other afflictions. This is purely a matter of public health: the licensing process could be made more complicated, perhaps, or at least informational, to assure that the owner has some idea of what is essential for a dog owner to provide. None of these suggestions would seem to be too much to ask—for public health reasons, but also because the results would almost surely be fewer miserable dogs.

# Canine Health Problems by Breed

The following list of breeds and the diseases to which they are more or less prone includes many of the commonly acquired breeds. Of course, this does not by any means suggest that all members of a breed are going to get all, or even one, of the diseases. (HD stands for Hip Dysplasia and PRA for Progressive Retinal Atrophy.)

| | |
|---|---|
| Afghan hound | HD, cataracts, paralysis |
| Airedale terrier | HD |
| Akita | HD, bad knees, thyroid problems |
| Alaskan Malamute | HD, skin disorders, thyroid problems |
| American cocker spaniel | PRA, cataracts, glaucoma, ear infections, heart disease, epilepsy |
| American Eskimo dog | HD, PRA |

| | |
|---|---|
| American Staffordshire terrier | HD, tumors |
| American Water spaniel | skin conditions |
| Australian Cattle Dog | HD, PRA, congenital deafness |
| Basenji | kidney disorder, eye problems |
| Basset hound | ear infections, disc problems |
| Beagle | hypothyroidism, hernia, epilepsy, spinal disc problems, HD |
| Bernese Mountain dog | HD, elbow dysplasia |
| Bloodhound | eye problems, HD |
| Boxer | corneal ulcers |
| Bullmastiff | HD, eyelid problems |
| Bull terrier | kneecap problems, deafness |
| Border collie | epilepsy, deafness, HD, PRA |
| Boston terrier | respiratory problems, cataracts |
| Bulldog | congenital heart disease |
| Cardigan Welsh Corgi | HD, PRA, eye problems |
| Collie | PRA, deafness |
| Chesapeake Bay retriever | HD, PRA, cataracts, eczema |
| Cairn terrier | skin allergies |
| Chow chow | HD, skin conditions, eyelid problems |
| Chihuahua | rheumatism, heart disease |
| Canaan Dog | NOT GIVEN TO HEALTH PROBLEMS |

| | |
|---|---|
| Chinese Sharpei | HD, eyelid problems, skin conditions |
| Dachshund | heart disease, spinal disc problems, diabetes, urinary stones |
| Doberman Pinscher | HD, heart disease, thyroid and liver problems |
| Dalmatian | deafness, HD, urinary stones |
| English cocker spaniel | PRA, eye problems, ear infections |
| English setter | deafness, HD |
| English Springer spaniel | HD, PRA, ear infections |
| Foxhound | NOT GIVEN TO HEALTH PROBLEMS |
| German shepherd | HD, gastric disorders, spinal paralysis |
| Golden retriever | HD, PRA, heart problems, cataracts, epilepsy |
| Great Dane | HD, bone cancer, heart disease |
| Great Pyrenees | HD, eyelid problems |
| Irish setter | HD, PRA, heart disease, epilepsy |
| Irish terrier | NOT GIVEN TO HEALTH PROBLEMS |
| Jack Russell terrier | glaucoma, PRA, epilepsy |
| Keeshond | HD, skin conditions, heart disease |
| Kerry Blue terrier | cysts, eye problems, tumors |
| Labrador retriever | HD, PRA, cataracts |

| | |
|---|---|
| Lhasa apso | Kidney problems, eye lacerations |
| Mastiff | Loose kneecap, hypoglycemia |
| Miniature pinscher | Mange, epilepsy |
| Miniature poodle | PRA, cataracts, glaucoma, eye and ear infections, digestive problems, heart disease, epilepsy |
| Newfoundland | HD, heart disease |
| Norfolk terrier | NOT GIVEN TO HEALTH PROBLEMS |
| Old English sheepdog | HD, cataracts, auto-immune problems |
| Pekingese | eye infections and lacerations, respiratory problems, collapsed nostrils, cleft palate, spinal disk problems |
| Pembroke Welsh Corgi | HD, eye problems |
| Pointer | HD, thyroid problems, dwarfism |
| Pomeranian | eye infections, collapsed windpipe, heart disease |
| Portuguese water dog | HD, PRA, neurological disorder |
| Pug | eye lacerations, eyeball popping out, collapsed nostril |
| Rhodesian Ridgeback | HD |

| | |
|---|---|
| Rottweiler | heart problems, HD, hypothyroidism elbow dysplasia |
| Saint Bernard | HD, heart disease, eyelid problems |
| Samoyed | HD, PRA, glaucoma, retinal problems |
| Scottish terrier | skin problems, jawbone disorders |
| Shih-tzu | slipped stifle (kneecap) eye lacerations, respiratory problems |
| Siberian Husky | HD, PRA, cataracts, corneal problems, hypothyroidism |
| Silky terrier | NOT GIVEN TO HEALTH PROBLEMS |
| Skye terrier | NOT GIVEN TO HEALTH PROBLEMS |
| Staffordshire bull terrier | cataracts, tumors |
| Standard poodle | Adrenal insufficiency, HD, PRA, cataracts |
| Standard schnauzer | HD |
| Tibetan spaniel | NOT GIVEN TO HEALTH PROBLEMS |
| Toy fox terrier | eye problems, skin problems |
| Toy Manchester terrier | slipped stifle (kneecap), bleeding disorders |
| Toy poodle | PRA, cataracts, glaucoma, eye and ear infections |

| | |
|---|---|
| Weimaraner | HD, bleeding disorder, tumors |
| West Highland white terrier | jawbone calcification, liver disease, hip arthritis |
| Yorkshire terrier | slipped stifle (kneecap) eye infections |

Many breeds are represented by local or state-wide rescue groups. You can look up a breed online and find such groups. Typically they provide information on breed health and other matters of interest.

*Appendix C*

# Trainability by Breed

Stanley Coren, psychologist at the University of British Columbia and an avid dog trainer as well as author of numerous very readable books about dogs, set out to rank breeds based on what he called their "working and obedience intelligence." After several frustrating false starts he hit on the idea of asking the opinions of those experts who judge obedience trials in North American dog shows. Obedience trials are designed primarily to produce dogs that have been trained to behave well in the home and elsewhere. He sent out fairly long and complex questionnaires to some 400-odd such experts and about half responded. Coren was pleased to find a considerable degree of agreement. For example, Coren writes, "190 of the 199 judges placed the border collie in the top ten!" And of the 199 judges, 121 ranked the Afghan hound at the bottom.

He was cautioned by many of the judges that none of this was to suggest that all members of a breed were the same.

Indeed, what was being specified here was essentially the difficulty of training dogs up to a certain level of competence. All breeds are trainable; it just takes a lot more work on the part of the trainer of some breeds. About mutts (which to be politically correct are called crossbreeds), Coren said that a rule of thumb is that the dog will rank about the same as the parent it most resembles. Once there is a great and impenetrable mixture, all bets are off.

Here, with Dr. Coren's kind permission, is his list of 140 breeds from the revised edition of his book, *The Intelligence of Dogs*.

These are the brightest in obedience training. Most dogs in these breeds learn commands fast—within five exposures—and then obey the first time given the command about 90 percent of the time.

1. Border collie
2. Poodle
3. German shepherd
4. Golden retriever
5. Doberman pinscher
6. Shetland sheepdog
7. Labrador retriever
8. Papillon
9. Rottweiler
10. Australian Cattle Dog

The dogs between 11 and 26 are all excellent working dogs, learning commands within five to fifteen exposures and remembering them well, though needing a bit of practice. They respond to first command about 85 percent of the time.

11. Pembroke Welsh Corgi
12. Miniature schnauzer
13. English springer spaniel
14. Belgian Tervuren
15. Schipperke, Belgian sheep dog
16. Collie, Keeshond
17. German short-haired pointer
18. Flat-coated retriever, English cocker spaniel, Standard schnauzer
19. Brittany spaniel
20. Cocker spaniel, Nova Scotia Duck Tolling retriever
21. Weimaraner
22. Belgian Malinois, Bernese Mountain dog
23. Pomeranian
24. Irish water spaniel
25. Vizsla
26. Cardigan Welsh Corgi

These, between 27 and 39, are above-average working dogs who may take as many as twenty-five exposures to learn a simple command. They need extra practice and will respond to the first command about 70 percent of the time.

27. Chesapeake Bay retriever, Puli, Yorkshire terrier
28. Giant schnauzer, Portuguese water dog
29. Airedale, Bouvier de Flandres
30. Border terrier, Briard
31. Welsh springer spaniel
32. Manchester terrier
33. Samoyed
34. Field spaniel, Newfoundland, Australian terrier, American Staffordshire terrier, Gordon setter, Bearded collie

35. American Eskimo dog, Cairn terrier, Kerry Blue terrier, Irish setter
36. Norwegian elkhound
37. Affenpinscher, Silky terrier, Miniature pinscher, English setter, Pharoah hound, Cumber spaniel
38. Norwich terrier
39. Dalmatian

Breeds ranking from 40 to 54 are average learners, taking twenty to forty-five repetitions to get up to snuff. In the absence of regular practice, they may forget. They respond to the first command about 50 percent of the time, and are especially sensitive to the distance of their trainers, becoming less and less responsive the farther away they are. They require excellent trainers or they can become "a mess."

40. Soft-coated Wheaten terrier, Bedlington terrier, Smooth-haired fox terrier
41. Curly-coated retriever, Irish wolfhound
42. Kuvasz, Australian shepherd
43. Saluki, Finnish spitz, pointer
44. Cavalier King Charles spaniel, German wirehaired pointer, Black-and-tan coonhound, American water spaniel
45. Siberian husky, Bichon frise, English toy spaniel
46. Greyhound, Harrier, Parson (formerly Jack) Russell terrier
47. West Highland white terrier, Havanese, Scottish deerhound
48. Boxer, Great Dane
49. Dachshund, Staffordshire bull terrier, Shiba Inu
50. Malamute

51. Whippet, Chinese Sharpei, Wire-haired fox terrier
52. Rhodesian Ridgeback
53  Ibizan hound, Welsh terrier, Irish terrier
54. Boston terrier, Akita

The group below are at best fair, requiring some twenty-five repetitions before they "begin to show any glimmering of understanding when presented with a new command." They need a lot of practice and refresher sessions, and often appear distracted. Expert trainers will get spotty behavior most of the time. These breeds are definitely not for first-time dog-owners.

55. Skye terrier
56. Norfolk terrier, Sealyham terrier
57. Pug
58. French bulldog
59. Brussels griffon, Maltese terrier
60. Italian greyhound
61. Chinese crested
62. Dandie Dinmont terrier, Vendeen, Tibetan terrier, Japanese chin, Lakeland terrier
63. Old English sheepdog
64. Great Pyrenees
65. Scottish terrier, Saint Bernard
66. Bull terrier, Petit Basset Griffon Vendeen
67. Chihuahua
68. Lhasa apso
69. Bullmastiff

These last ten breeds are the most difficult to train. It can take forty to fifty repetitions before they have any idea what they should do. A hundred repetitions are not unusual and then the dog may forget the exercise altogether. When they do respond to commands, they give the appearance of being displeased. Even expert trainers have a terrible time with these breeds.

I have heard someone justify the beagle's typical inattentiveness to training as being the result of their especially good nose: any new smell will distract them from the business at hand.

70. Shih-tzu
71. Basset hound
72. Mastiff, beagle
73. Pekingese
74. Bloodhound
75. Borzoi
76. Chow chow
77. Bulldog
78. Basenji
79. Afghan hound

Another source of behavioral rankings, as noted in the text, is the Harts' book, *The Perfect Puppy*, (see bibliography).

*Appendix D*

# The Wild Dogs
# of the World

## Foxes

More fox species roam the world than any other canid—in all, twenty-one (or twenty-two) species of fox out of the thirty-four (or thirty-five) wild canid species. As a general rule, foxes are comparatively small (up to thirty pounds but typically smaller), with longish, sharp muzzles, thin legs, and long bushy tails. Foxes are also, corporately, the most cosmopolitan of canids, occurring on every continent but Antarctica. The most cosmopolitan of all is the red fox, scientifically thought of as *Vulpes vulpes*, which literally means the Fox fox or, one assumes, the quintessential fox.

The largest of the foxes, reaching as much as thirty pounds though usually lighter by a third, the red fox evolved originally in Eurasia and is found in practically every part of that great land mass, as well as two ranges in northern Africa. In the seventeenth century, men bent on fox hunting introduced it to the eastern United States, and a century or so later, the

Australians brought some there to attempt to control an exploding population of rabbits they also had ill-advisedly brought to their shores. A few red foxes have been imported into Polynesia where they have no doubt wiped out most of the native creatures.

Red foxes are mostly but not all red in color. Small numbers have black bellies, or a black cross on their backs, or are all black, and some are all white except for a few gray markings. Those red foxes from upland areas have coats that are a bright golden red, while those nearer sea level have a paler, more yellow coat. There is also the silver variety which we met in chapter three.

Red foxes prefer not to live in the neighborhood of wolves or coyotes, who prey on them, or in dense forests or deserts, though some do live in an extremely arid part of India. They also are perfectly at home in towns and even big cities where they are free of most predators, including human ones. The red fox is so common in London and other British cities that Brits who want to keep them out of their gardens can now, according to *New Scientist* magazine, buy fox repellents that emit an ultrasonic sound. The packaging of this useful device warns "This product will not work with deaf foxes."

Normally red fox society consists of a mating pair and, in many cases, a couple or more daughters who help raise the next generation. (This is, indeed, the common social situation for most fox species.) Since about 30 percent of the overall red fox population are nonmating vixens (females) and nonmating dog foxes (males), a lot of foxes can be killed without unduly upsetting the reproduction potential of the group.

To make their continuing survival all the more likely, they are extremely opportunistic feeders. Their chief food is mice and voles, upon whom they pounce like cats, but they are true omnivores, taking anything from insects to the young of wild boars or deer, from human garbage to what a domestic dog leaves in its dish. They are aided as nocturnal hunters chiefly by their astoundingly acute hearing: evidently they can hear a mouse in the grass of a meadow from about 150 feet. It is virtually impossible to approach a red fox unnoticed, and it is very difficult to catch one. If threatened, they can run at up to thirty miles an hour for considerable distance; they can broad-jump a distance of six feet and leap normal fences; they are good swimmers, and are known to take to the water to put a pursuer off their track. Indeed, from Aesop's fables to the European folk tales of Reynard the Fox to Brer Fox of Uncle Remus, storytellers have been altogether correct to characterize this most familiar and common fox as clever, crafty, and capable of wonderful feats of mischief and escape.

The other common North American *Vulpes* is called the swift fox (*Vulpes velox*), and includes several subspecies some of which were formerly called kit foxes. Inhabitants of the Western states, all the swift foxes are chiefly carnivorous, taking rabbits and rodents, but they are small enough themselves to be taken by hawks. They are not especially territorial and do not scent-mark their home bases. They get together in pairs for the mating season, and the males feed the vixens until the kits are weaned. It appears that they are extending their ranges back into northern states like Montana and some of the Canadian provinces.

*Swift fox*

The only other notable fox of North America is the gray fox (*Urocyon cinereoargenteus*) which means (clumsily, even bewilderingly) ash-colored silver taildog. The gray fox is found from southern Canada all the way south to Venezuela, but it is not gray. Its coat is part a grizzled black and white and part a light orange. It has a thick body, relatively short legs, and oval-shaped pupils, unlike the slit-shaped pupils of the *Vulpes* species. Nocturnal, it seems to mate for life, and will eat whatever is available. One place in the United States where it rarely is seen is on the open plains where there are no trees. The gray fox has strong hooked claws on its feet and uses them to climb trees. Many nest in trees—as high up as thirty feet— and will retreat into a tree when imperiled.

The smallest of all the canids, the Fennec fox (*Vulpes zerda*) stands about eight inches high at the shoulder and weighs between two and three pounds. In other words, it is smaller than the rabbits it occasionally takes. Fennec is a version of the Arab word for fox—*fanak*—and zerda is evidently a corruption of the Greek *xeri*, meaning dry. Indeed, the Fennec fox is fully adapted to life in the deserts of North Africa, being generally light-colored to reflect the sun's heat, and possessed of a thick under-coat to protect against the desert's frigid nights. In addition, the pads of their feet are covered with hair, which protects against the burning heat underfoot as well as providing good traction in the loose sand. And their ears are immense, some six inches long—indeed, the largest compared to their heads of any canid. Large ears not only help in hunting but permit excess body heat to dissipate. Finally, like many desert animals, they can get along with little water, their kidneys capable of keeping water loss by urine to a minimum.

*Fennec foxes*

They generally survive on small desert rodents like gerbils and on lizards, insects, and bird eggs. Also they dig for roots, which provide moisture as well. They are fairly social, sometimes living in extended family groups rather than in mating pairs only. Once a pair has a litter, the female becomes highly aggressive in defense, and the male, while providing food for his mate, never crosses the den's threshold.

Of the other *Vulpes* species, less is known. *Vulpes chama* lives on arid South African savannahs, a small, housecat-sized fox with big ears and a long bushy tail. It hunts nocturnally, has an omnivorous diet, and lives in pairs. Two other African species who habituate dry regions are *Vulpes ruepelli* in North Africa and *Vulpes pallida* in Somalia and Sudan. Little is known about these two; that is also the case for *Vulpes bengalensis*, an orange fox from India, Nepal, and Pakistan; *Vulpes ferrilata*, a small fox that lives above 16,000 feet in Tibet; and *Vulpes cana*, a nocturnal and solitary whitish fox of southern Russia.

In South America, six foxes are called zorros and are members of a genus formerly known as *Dusicyon*, which means foolish dog. What was deemed foolish about these six zorro species is not clear, but the genus name was recently changed to another pejorative, *Pseudolopex*, which means false fox. What is false about these six species is not clear either. Taxonomists do get details wrong from time to time, but this sounds more like a deliberate put-down of Latin America, and I for one am scandalized. As for getting things wrong, one of the zorros is the Pampas zorro, or *Pseudolopex gymnocereus*. What that means is false fox with a hairless tail. But the Pampas zorro has a bushy tail like most foxes around the world. Even back in the days of *Dusicyon*, this zorro was falsely described as having a hairless tail. So why, when the taxonomists were changing the genus name, didn't they change the obviously fallacious species name? Someone should come forward and straighten this all out.

In any event, the thoroughly (scientifically) misnamed Pampas zorro is a creature of the lowland prairies, deserts, and woodlands of central South America, and is highly carnivorous though with a bit of a sweet tooth, going for melons and sugarcane on occasion. It is solitary, nocturnal, and has two unusual, even slightly bizarre—in fact, maybe a little foolish—habits. This zorro is known to collect useless bits of cloth and leather and put them in their dens. Also, when confronted by a human, it will freeze, lying down and shutting its eyes. This no doubt makes things easier for hunters who kill them for their fur and because they do occasionally go after lambs.

Of the other pseudofoxes of South America, not a great deal is known besides their names and habitats. Most of them are small, grayish, and typically nocturnal. The Culpeo (*Pseudolopex culpaeus*) is the continent's largest fox, a hunter mainly of rabbits and hares, who will take young lambs and vegetable matter as well. Its habitat is a long strip stretching from Ecuador south to southern Chile. It is unique, so far as foxes are concerned, in having what is called a hierarchical matriarchy. In other words, the females fight for dominance and make the big-time decisions, such as mating and moving from one place to another.

Two other foxes of South America stand out. One is the Crab-eating Fox (*Cerdocyon thous*), who lives in open country from northern South America as far south as Argentina. Contrary to its common name, it will eat anything that is available (including land crabs). It lives in pairs, is not particularly territorial, and is thought of as common, unthreatened, bold, and opportunistic. It is happy to use the dens of other creatures and, indeed, seems to be the most laid-back of foxes. Its genus name means crafty dog, and its species name means jackal (which it resembles).

The Amazon rain forest is home to the Small-eared zorro (*Atelocynos microtis*), a stocky, short-legged creature with a long muzzle and partially webbed feet. It requires undisturbed rain forest and prefers to live near watercourses. It is largely carnivorous, eating fish, small mammals, and insects. Because of habitat destruction in the Amazon, this fox is severely threatened. Its species name, *microtis*, is straightforward enough, meaning small-eared,

*Small-eared fox*

but its genus name is yet another gratuitous nomenclatural slap: imperfect dog. It would seem, on the contrary, to be pretty well adapted to the watery areas of the Amazon, what with its partially webbed feet.

Yet another linguistic gaffe occurred in the naming of Africa's Bat-eared fox: *Otocyon megalotis* literally means Eardog big-eared. How about big-eared termite-eater, for this fox does eat mostly termites as well as a lot of other insects? It is unique among canids in having two extra molars for grinding up the exoskeletons of insects.

The only fox that has evolved to live in the bone-chilling wastes above the Arctic Circle is the Arctic fox, (*Alopex lagopus*, meaning hare-footed fox). It comes in two winter colors, white and blue. The white ones inhabit the main areas of its circumpolar range, while the quite rare blue ones are found along the edges of the range. In summer, the white morph turns grayish, while the blue morph becomes chocolate brown. The winter coat includes a thick undercoat that has the highest insulation value of any mammalian coat. Other adaptations to the cold are small rounded ears that give off a minimum of body heat, and hair-covered feet that prevent frostbite.

*Bat-eared foxes*

The Arctic fox is an opportunistic hunter, but depends to a great extent on lemmings for food. Indeed, these foxes and the lemmings are engaged in strict minuet of population rise and fall that has been going on for thousands of years, if not longer. The lemmings increase to a peak population every four years and the foxes do the same, reaching a peak at the same time or just thereafter. Then their numbers jointly descend.

Even though they have been hunted for their fur to the point of persecution, the Arctic fox holds little fear of humans. There are plenty of stories about them coming right into camps in daylight and in plain view swiping food. They are perhaps the most peripatetic of all foxes, one of them being known to have traveled nearly a thousand miles from its birthplace.

## Large Wild Dogs

The big wild dogs—jackals, hunting dogs, and coyotes (as well as wolves)—have often gotten a bad rap from people who dwell in what is claimed to be civilization. One of the most appalling international terrorists of the twentieth century was known as Carlos the Jackal. The ancient Egyptians had a jackal-headed god, Anubis, who led the dead into the underworld, and thereafter innumerable cultures have associated jackals, who are frequent scavengers, with death, not to mention cowardice. (It has always puzzled me that humans tend to be so disgusted by scavengers, eating dead animals and all. Most humans eat dead animals, too).

Many Americans—and especially the preponderance of agricultural folk in the West—still hold the view that wolves and coyotes are dangerous, even lethal to humans, never mind livestock, and should all be eliminated. In fact, in late 2005,

Canadian police attributed the death of a man by mauling to a wolf, and if that was the truly the case, it was the first North American wolf-caused human death in decades, if ever. Europeans and Americans have come very close to success in ridding their worlds of wolves, and American government agents and ranchers have been trying for more than a hundred years to do the same with coyotes—to no avail whatsoever. In fact, in the coyote's case, there has been an astonishing instance of what is called blowback, as we shall see.

## Hunting Dogs

Probably fewer than one in 10,000 Americans have ever heard of a canid called the Dhole, but it is native to an enormous region in southeastern Asia, from Mongolia south to Malaysia and from India east to the Pacific Ocean. Known to science as *Cuon alpinus* (mountain dog), the Dhole weighs up to forty pounds (or more) and lives and hunts in family packs, bringing down large prey such as small and large deer, antelopes, wild pigs, goats and sheep, birds, and even monkeys. These canids look much like domestic dogs, reddish or tawny and white underneath, with erect but slightly rounded ears and a short, wide snout that makes for powerful bites, though nothing like the crushing bite a big cat like a leopard or tiger can administer.

A hunting pack of Dholes brings down its prey by tearing bites off the fleeing animal, in essence eating it alive, and this has led to a great deal of prejudice among humans. An old Dhole hand, naturalist E. R. C. Davidar, wrote in 1975 that until recently, most studies of the Dhole "were made along the sights of rifles." In fact, the Dhole adjusts its hunting tactics to the prey and terrain at hand, silently running down the big sambar deer for example, but charging other smaller prey in a sudden burst of speed. They tend to take turns feeding at a large kill, and are especially amicable among themselves. Dholes are known to go after some livestock, but they far prefer their usual wild prey. They present no danger to people, except in the case of an individual Dhole with rabies.

These are highly social animals, with packs occasionally and temporarily reaching as many as forty in some canid form of a jamboree, later splitting back into smaller packs. In some instances, gravid females will share a den and raise their pups jointly. The entire pack—more often from five to twelve adults, typically related—provide food for the pups, regurgitating for them after a hunt, during which some adults remain near the den as guards. They communicate with each other with all the vocalizations of domestic dogs except loud barking. They howl, snarl, growl, whine and whimper, and yap, but they also whistle. The naturalist Davidar said the whistle could be "imitated by blowing into a medium bore rifle cartridge with a series of three short toots."

Little is known about the size of populations of these much-maligned canids, but they are declining throughout much of their ancient range and are considered endangered. They do tend to be especially susceptible to canine distemper, which is carried into their midst from time to time by both jackals and domestic village dogs.

Much more widely known and far more assiduously studied is the African wild dog (or Cape hunting dog) known as *Lycaon pictus*, the Greek word for wolf being cobbled together with Latin for painted. Of course, it isn't a wolf, but the idea of paint is apt, for this canid has a blotchy coat of black, white, yellow, and brown in no particular pattern—each individual being differently adorned. They do all have a black muzzle and large, oval-shaped black ears, and at first sight look a little like hyenas. Strong long legs enable these dogs to average more than thirty miles per hour over long stretches. If there is such an emotion as dismay felt by the likes of wildebeests and gazelles, it may reach its extreme when they notice that a pack of some 100 African wild dogs out on patrol has turned their way. Someone (or some ones) will soon be run down at speeds of up to forty-five miles per hour, and totally consumed within minutes. As in the case of the Dhole, this means of feeding themselves has earned the African wild dog a bad reputation among some people.

African wild dog

Once a pack of some hundred sets out after prey, it rarely fails, but packs that large are rare today since most of these animals are now sequestered in parks where distances are less and prey are fewer. The largest packs one sees today are in the neighborhood of thirty animals, and concern exists among wildlife biologists that such small packs may in the long run prove unsustainable. African wild dogs once ranged throughout sub-Saharan Africa, but now live in restricted zones south of Sudan and down to the tip of the continent, mostly in savannah and other arid lands. The largest populations are found in southern Africa—notably Botswana, Namibia, and Zimbabwe. On the other hand, the Serengeti may be the hunting dog's best hope. A population there was wiped out in 1991 by a rabies epidemic (so social are the wild dogs that no one escapes such diseases once underway). But antirabies campaigns in the surround have eliminated the source of rabies in the Serengeti and a wild population of some forty individuals has taken up residence there—a 25,000 square-mile area that is free of livestock farmers.

A pack consists of an alpha male and female who alone mark the boundaries of the pack's territory, and are the only mating pair. All the rest, usually relatives, help with the raising of the next generation. Separate hierarchies exist for male and female pack members, and one's rank is settled in a way unknown in other canids. Aggressive posturing is rare, and actual fights more so. Instead, these ferocious, terrestrial piranhas of the plains maintain order by submission. Such large amounts of food are required by the pack—and the large litters of the alpha pair, often up to some twenty pups—that cooperation is essential. When two of these wild dogs meet, they lick each others' muzzles, whine, even regurgitate some food for the other—in a sense, they act like puppies, flattening their ears and lowering their front quarters, which is, typically among canids, an invitation to play. Indeed, when not hunting, resting or sleeping (which they do in a great jumble), they spend a lot of time and energy playing.

## Jackals

An Asian folktale tells of how the jackal goes forth and scares up game animals which the lion then kills and feeds on, and then shares the rest with the helpful jackal. This is a refreshing antidote to the more common jackal-as-coward, jackal-and-death motifs, but also in at least one recorded instance it actually happened. In Kenya, a female black-backed jackal was observed several times running in and among a game herd, which enabled a cheetah to move in closer than it otherwise could have done. Once it made a successful kill, she and her offspring fed on the carcass and then turned it over to the jackal.

The black-backed jackal (*Canis mesomelasis* or black-middled dog) is one of four jackal species who are mostly confined to Africa (though one ranges into Europe as far west as Italy and into Asia as far east as Thailand). The black-backed jackal lives from the Gulf of Aden into Tanzania and, in a separate population, in southern Africa. Weighing anything from fifteen to thirty pounds, it looks like a long-legged fox with a bushy tail. It is slender, golden in color with a highly distinctive black and silver "saddle."

Sometimes thought of as the coyotes of Africa, these jackals prefer open grassland, eating practically anything, and also preferring the path of least work and resistance when it comes to obtaining food. They often scavenge lion, leopard, and hyena kills, and when they must, they hunt gazelles and the calves of larger ungulates, as well as rodents, hares, and insects. They are said to be 75 percent successful when they hunt Thompson's gazelles. In other words, they are very good at what they do, which is why they are so successful.

Monogamous—for up to eight years—pairs are extremely close, engaging in most activities together with a good deal of mutual grooming. They form small packs more often than not—the mating pair and some earlier offspring who act as helpers, bringing up the pups. The young jackals engage in fairly fierce dominance battles, with the most dominant ones eventually leaving the pack and its one-square-mile territory to form their own. These jackals are quite vocal: they yell, woof, whine, growl, and howl to communicate with one another.

More widely distributed in Africa is the Side-striped Jackal (*Canis adustus*, meaning, for some reason, the sunburned dog). It has pale stripes along its side and is grayish brown with a white-tipped tail. It ranges throughout central and southern Africa, in woodlands and the more humid parts of the African savannahs. Unlike the black-backed jackal, this one is mostly nocturnal, does less scavenging, *Side-stripped jackal* and preys on small mammals like hares and rodents, as well as eating insects and a good deal of fruit. They are monogamous and form small packs, presumably similar to the black-backed jackal. To communicate at night, they do not howl but cry loudly.

The most cosmopolitan jackal is *Canis aureus*, the Golden jackal. The one that ranges into Europe and Asia as well as throughout north Africa, they prefer desert and other dry habitat. The coat is grayish yellow, or golden, or red, and their diet consists of half plant matter and half animal matter, the latter being rabbits, rodents, insects, birds, and the young of herbivores. Like the others, the Golden jackal is monogamous, living in breeding pairs with earlier offspring serving as helpers. Again, like the others, the Golden pairs are highly cooperative and call to each other when separated. They have a very distinctive howl: a high-pitched sound that carries for miles and serves to keep them together, reinforce their relationship, and also alert others to their claim of territory. Their howl, by the way, is considered an ill omen among some Indian tribespeople.

Jackals, all of which are smaller than the hunting dogs, more closely resemble foxes, differing mainly in the larger prey they are capable of taking, in their greater reliance on carrion, and their tendency to live in small packs, while foxes lean toward the more solitary life.

One other "jackal" lives in two small ranges above 10,000 feet in Ethiopia, where it is severely threatened with extinction. The Simien jackal (*Canis simiensis*) it is quite tame, which makes it vulnerable to hunters. Larger than the other jackals, it weighs up to almost forty pounds, and has a longer muzzle with smaller teeth. Ninety percent of its diet is mole rats. Not very much is known about it, and many wildlife biologists believe that it is more closely related to wolves and (long ago) coyotes than to jackals.

## The One and Only Coyote

In the long epic that is the Navajo Indian creation story, First Man set out to order the universe, and an urgent task was to put the stars into the nighttime firmament. Methodically, he placed the stars in certain patterns, producing seven constellations such as the Pleiades and Orion. While he rested, a figure known as Coyote happened by and saw First Man's pile of stars on the ground. Being an irrepressible troublemaker, he picked them up and threw them willy-nilly into the sky. This is why, the Navajos say, there are seven constellations up there amid what is otherwise a twinkling chaos.

Coyote—part animal, part human, part god—is the quintessential Trickster, the shape-changing mischief-maker with bawdy appetites. He is the sometime incompetent, like the cartoon character who always fails to catch the Road Runner. But he is also a creator, and sometimes all too effective, inventing both lies and death. Coyote always has some hidden agenda—often revolving around food or sex. Among the Indian tribes of the American Southwest in particular, he is the flim-flam man, the con artist. This is a role played in other parts of the continent by the Raven, the Hare, and a Spider, a role that is probably very ancient in human affairs, a role akin to the shaman who can both heal and kill.

The name coyote derives from the Aztec word *coyotl*, which means barking dog, as does its scientific name, *Canis latrans*. Ranchers in the United States and Canada have long considered it the most contemptible of vermin, to be hunted, tortured, poisoned, eradicated—but eradication has worked only locally

Coyote

and only for short periods. Everywhere the coyote has bounced back, even extended it range—except where wolves still live or have been reintroduced. The coyote is nothing if not flexible, adaptable, and opportunistic. It is now the most successful and widespread predator on the North American continent.

One may think of the coyote as the Swiss Army knife of the genus *Canis*. They are sufficiently large that, as a small pack, they can bring down fairly large prey like deer, even the occasional elk, but they can survive perfectly well hunting solo, pouncing on mice and voles and other small rodents, even catching insects. They can hunt during the day or at night, though they tend to be nocturnal. They can live in the arid country of the Southwest, the cold of Alaska, the brushy wetlands of Minnesota, and in the subtropical forests of Central America.

In the Southwest, they are typically a yellowish color, but darker on higher ground, in the north, and in the east. They come in various sizes—from some thirty-five pounds to seventy-five. Their cubs are born in a den, usually one excavated by some other animal, and the male provides food for the mother and the cubs for four months, when the little ones begin to learn to catch their own food—starting with insects. Male yearlings will typically leave home first, setting out for other territories, leaving some young females to help with the next season's cubs in some instances. Packs will assemble and break apart, apparently depending on the availability of prey.

Those coyotes who have come to live in towns and cities in close proximity to humans are known to include in their diet small pets, especially house cats, which does not go down well with people who don't bring their pets in at night. Of course, coyotes also take livestock, particularly young sheep, but no assay of a coyote's stomach contents has ever shown that they rely heavily on domestic animals. At most, about 8 percent of some coyotes' diet is livestock, the rest being largely rodents and carrion. Nonetheless, their reputation as 1) sheep and cow killers and 2) competitors with sport hunters for deer and elk led the United States government and most Western states and counties, beginning in the nineteenth century, to try to wipe them off the planet. Such programs became a kind of madness. In 1960, the state of Arizona spent $157, 603 to kill 1,864 coyotes, while the value of livestock and pets killed that same year by coyotes added up to $42,225. A great deal of the effort depended on poisoning carcasses, but finally by 1972, this was forbidden on U.S. public land, since it also tended to poison every other creature in the neighborhood.

One of the more telling incidents in the extermination wars occurred in Klamath County, Oregon, in the 1940s. A program developed whereby every coyote in the county—more than 10,000—was killed for the benefit of the county's farmlands. But soon there arose what came to be known as the Mouse War. The mouse population exploded, to the point where estimates said there were 10,000 mice *per acre.* Vast sums were soon spent to get control of the mouse population, and soon the county was reintroducing coyotes.

It seems in each instance where governments and private citizens tried to kill or drive out the coyote population, the coyotes responded by increasing the sizes of their litters— from the typical four or six to as many as nineteen—and sent more young coyotes out into new territory. There is evidence as well that once governments take the pressure off coyote populations, they drop somewhat. Today, this species, once confined to the Western states and provinces and to northern Mexico, has extended its range into every state in the United States except Hawaii and, wags like to say, as soon as they invent boats they'll get there, too. Today, you can live in the suburbs of Boston and in the canyons of Los Angles and hear coyotes howl.

In March of 2006, a coyote was seen in New York City's Central Park and eventually rounded up and shipped elsewhere. Coyotes in crowded Manhattan were considered highly unusual and may in fact be so. But maybe not. Eastern and Midwestern cities seem to have a lot more coyote residents than they previously imagined. The case of Chicago stands out. There, Stanley Gerht of Ohio State University has been tracking and studying the city's coyotes since 2001, and has found not the several dozen that were estimated but somewhere between several hundred and a couple of thousand. They live in large packs (for territorial defense) but typically hunt alone. One of their targets is the eggs of Canada geese, who had been proliferating in the city but are now under control. The urban coyotes tend to live longer than their rural kin, and pose little threat to humans. Trouble can arise if people feed them, however inadvertently. The city populations tend to be strictly nocturnal, more so than rural ones, and thus their considerable presence has gone largely unnoticed until Gerht's study.

Coyotes can and do hybridize with wolves and domestic dogs. The red wolf, an endangered species in North America, is believed to be the result of ancient wolf-coyote hybridization, and some suspect that the large Eastern coyote is also a hybrid—with domesticated dogs. I'd be willing to bet the farm that our two extremely nervous Rez dogs—the sleek

Doberman–Navajo sheep dog cross, and the yellow Hopi dog—have some relatively recent coyote genes in them. Rez dogs live a largely feral life on the edges of human habitation, and there are plenty of coyotes in the neighborhood. And both our Rez dogs are weird, especially watchful and nervous.

Relatively secretive, coyotes are in fact known to most people only from the their nighttime howling sessions (suppressed, it seems, in cities), beginning with a chorus of high-pitched yips and then an eerie ensemble of yet higher-pitched howls, each voice singing a different series of notes. It is a primeval, almost scary performance.

My own experience with coyotes includes a time when Susanne and I lived on a high sand mesa overlooking the Rio Grande Valley in New Mexico, and a pair of coyotes moved into a preexisting burrow about a hundred feet away from our house on the far side of a steep arroyo that separated us from our neighbor. We were unaware of the coyotes' usurpation of the burrow (which had in earlier summers been the home of burrowing owls) until one night at about eight o'clock when we noticed five tawny little coyote pups playing near the burrow entrance. They rolled around on each other, barely able to walk, pushing and falling like so many two-week-old dog puppies.

The burrowing owls had taken to another burrow some fifty feet uphill, and they stood in a row of five watching the coyote puppies with their perpetually grumpy owlish frowns. Our two horses stood at the edge of the arroyo, staring at the romping coyotes, as did our dogs—and, of course, we too. For three weeks thereafter, every night at exactly five past eight, the puppies emerged and played for about fifteen minutes, then went in for the night, a predictable little pageant carefully observed by the owls, horses, dogs, us, and occasionally neighbors. After a week or so, the coyotes would pay no attention when Susanne approached within about fifty feet to photograph them. Then one night they all disappeared. We learned later that coyote parents move their pups from one den to another quite often, to avoid parasites, disease, and snakes or other predators, so we did not take their departure personally.

# ACKNOWLEDGMENTS

The bibliography that follows is, of course, a list of the people whose work I have relied upon in writing most of this book and to them I am profoundly grateful, most especially to Stanley Coren whose insights into canid arcane are wonderful and who was kind enough to write a preface for someone he had never met.

The people at Smithsonian Books/Collins have made me feel right at home again in the folds of my former employer on the Washington Mall. Elisabeth Dyssegaard, the executive editor, has played an especially creative role, gently helping me see the proper shape of the book, encouraging both me and my wife Susanne, a photographer, to illustrate it, and inviting me to include my own observations of our six fellow travelers. The most important professional connection a writer can ever make is with an editor like Elisabeth. She is abetted by Dan Crissman, an administrative hero, and Amy Vreeland, the senior production editor who, with copyeditor

Suzanne Fass, magically made sure the text is as internally consistent as it is. Chris Welch, the book designer, did exactly what Elisabeth said she wanted when we first discussed this effort. "I want it," she said, "to be a beautiful book."

None of this would have happened were it not for Joe Regal, the singing literary agent, and his fellow denizens at Regal Literary. Joe is a long-term, deeply trusted friend of mine who never seems fazed by the often wayward affairs of the protean world of book publishing.

Finally, of course, I am indebted to the lady to whom practically all my books including this one have been dedicated, and to the six dogs (and their predecessors) who have filled my life with dog hair and, more often than not, joy.

# BIBLIOGRAPHY

Abrantes, Roger. *Dog Language*. Naperville, IL: Wakan Tanka Publishers, 1997.

Alderton, David. *Foxes, Wolves and Wild Dogs of the World*. New York: Facts on File, 1994.

Bekoff, Marc. *Minding Animals*. New York: Oxford University Press, 2002.

————. *The Emotional Lives of Animals*. Novato, California: New World Library, 2007.

———— and John A. Byers, eds. *Animal Play: Evolutionary, Comparative, and Ecological Perspectives*. Cambridge and New York: Cambridge University Press, 1998.

Clutton-Brock, Juliet. *A Natural History of Domesticated Animals*. Cambridge: Cambridge University Press, 1999.

Colbert, Edwin H. *Evolution of the Vertebrates*. New York: John Wiley & Sons, 1980.

Coleman, Jon T. *Vicious: Wolves and Men in America*. Yale University Press, New Haven: Yale University Press, 2004.

Coppinger, Raymond and Lorna Coppinger. *Dogs: A New Understanding of Canine Origin, Behavior, and Evolution*. Chicago: University of Chicago Press, 2001.

Coren, Stanley. *The Pawprints of History*. New York: Free Press, 2002.

————. *How Dogs Think*. Free Press, New York: Free Press, 2004.

Crockford, Susan J. "Native Dog Types in North America Before Arrival of European Dogs." Oral presentation at World Small Animal Veterinary Association Congress, Mexico City, 2005.

———. *Rhythms of Life: Thyroid Hormone & the Origin of Species.* Victoria, BC: Trafford Publishing, 2006.

———, B. Letchford, and C. Moyer. "Osteometric vs. genetic characterization of the Tahltan Bear Dog." In *Transitions in Zooarchaeology: New Methods and New Results,* Canadian Zooarchaeology Supplement #1. K. M. Stewart and F. L. Stewart, editors, 18–39. Ottawa: Canadian Museum of Nature, 2005.

Darwin, Charles. *The Expression of the Emotions in Man and Animals.* Chicago: University of Chicago Press, 1965.

Derr, Mark. *Dog's Best Friend: Annals of the Dog-Human Relationship.* Chicago: University of Chicago Press, 2004.

———. *A Dog's History of America.* New York: North Point Press, 2004.

Fagen, Robert. *Animal Play Behavior.* New York: Oxford University Press, 1981.

Fogle, Bruce. *The Dog's Mind.* New York: Howell Book House, 1990.

Fox, M. W., ed. *The Wild Canids: Their Systematics, Behavioral Ecology and Evolution.* New York: Van Nostrand Reinhold Company, 1975.

Gaita, Raimond. *The Philosopher's Dog.* New York: Random House, 2002.

Grady, Wayne. *The World of the Coyote.* San Francisco: Sierra Club Books, 1994.

Grandin, Temple and Catherine Johnson. *Animals in Translation.* New York: Scribner, 2005.

Hare, Brian, et al. "The Domestication of Social Cognition in Dogs." *Science* 298 (22 November 2002).

Hart, Benjamin L. and Lynnete A. *The Perfect Puppy.* New York: W. H. Freeman and Company, 1988.

Hausman, Gerald and Loretta. *The Mythology of Dogs.* New York: St. Martins Griffin, 1997.

Hempel, Amy and Jim Shepard. *Unleashed: Poems by Writers' Dogs.* New York: Three Rivers Press, 1995.

Houpt, Katherine A. *Domestic Animal Behavior.* Oxford: Blackwell Publishing, 2005.

Humphrey, Nicholas. *A History of Mind: Evolution and the Birth of Consciousness.* New York: Simon & Schuster, 1992.

————. *Seeing Red: A Study in Consciousness*. Cambridge, MA: The Belknap Press of Harvard University Press, 2006.

Leach, Maria, ed. *Funk & Wagnalls Standard Dictionary of Folklore, Mythology and Legend*. New York: Funk & Wagnalls, 1972.

Loendorf, Lawrence L. and Nancy Medaris Stone. *Mountain Spirit: The Sheep Eater Indians of Yellowstone*. Salt Lake City: The University of Utah Press, 2006.

Lopez, Barry. *Wolves and Men*, New York: Scribners, 1978.

MacDonald, D. W. and C. Sillero-Zubiri. *Biology and Conservation of Wild Canids*. New York: Oxford University Press, 2004.

Mech, L. David. *The Wolf: The Ecology and Behavior of an Endangered Species*. Garden City, NY: The Natural History Press, 1970.

————. *The Arctic Wolf*. Stillwater, MN: The Voyageur Press, 1988.

Millan, Cesar. *Cesar's Way*, New York: Harmony Books, 2006.

Morris, Desmond. *Dog Watching*. New York: Crown Publishers, 1986.

Owings, Donald H. and Eugene S. Morton. *Animal Vocal Communication: A New Approach*. Cambridge: Cambridge University Press, 1998.

Palmer, John. *The Illustrated Encyclopedia of Dog Breeds*. Wellfleet, MA: The Wellfleet Press, 1994.

Roth, Melinda. *The Man Who Talked to Dogs*. New York: Thomas Dunne Books, 2002.

Ryden, Hope. *God's Dog*. New York: Lyons & Burford, Publishers, 1979.

Scott, John Paul and John L. Fuller. *Genetics and the Social Behavior of the Dog*, Chicago: University of Chicago Press, 1965.

Schwartz, Marion. *A History of Dogs in the Early Americas*. New Haven: Yale University Press, 1997.

Serpell, James. *In the Company of Animals*. Oxford: Basil Blackwell Ltd., 1986.

————, ed. *The Domestic Dog: Its Evolution, Behaviour, and Interactions with People*. Cambridge: Cambridge University Press, 1995.

Smith, Douglas W., and Gary Ferguson. *Decade of the Wolf: Returning the Wild to Yellowstone*. Guilford, CT: The Lyons Press, 2005.

Thomas, Elizabeth Marshall. *The Hidden Life of Dogs*. Houghton Mifflin, Boston and New York: Houghton Mifflin, 1993.

Thurston, Mary Elizabeth, *The Lost History of the Canine Race*. Kansas City, MO: Andrews and McMeel, 1996.

Trut, Lyudmila N. "Early Canid Domestication: The Farm-Fox Experiment." *American Scientist* 87 (March-April 1991).

# INDEX

Page numbers in *italics* indicate illustrations.

Puget Sound, 76
punishment, learning and, 155–56,
    170
pupil (eye part), 110–11, 112–13
puppies, 89–99, 102, 105–6, 124,
    126
    play and, 93, 94, 96–97, 136, 142,
        163
    weaning of, 94, 97
puppies, coyote, 207–8
puppy mills, 82
pure-breds, 69, 77, 82–85

rabies, 81, 198, 199
raccoon dog, 16, *16*
raccoons, 10, 14
rats, 144, 145, 160, 165
reactivity, 152
reasoning, 149, 163–64
receptor nerves, touch, 102–3
red fox, 29, 189–91
red wolf, 23–24, 206
reflection, thought and, 162
rehoming, puppies and, 94–95
REM sleep, 149–50
Renaissance, 70–71
reptiles, 137
retina, 60, 92, 111–13, 114
retrievers, 81, 111, 158, 178, 179,
    184, 185
rewards, learning and, 155, 170
Rez dogs, 60–63, 206–7
rheas, 17
Rhodesian Ridgeback, 54, 172,
    180
*Rhythms of Life, The* (Crockford), 50
rice, 41
Rico (dog), 156–57
Rock and Great Basin, *74*
Rock Creek Park (Washington, D.
    C.), 24
rodents, 3, 17, 117
rods (eye part), 112–13
rolling over, 130
Roman Catholic Church, 70
Romanes, G. J., 108–9

Rome, ancient, 68
Rottweiler, 69, 82, 111, 131
    biting propensity of, 172
    health problems of, 181
    trainability ranking of, 184
Royal British Columbia Museum
    (Victoria), 76
Royal Society for the Prevention of
    Cruelty to Animals, 71
Runyon, Damon, 62
Russia, 23

Saint Bernard, 69, 181
Salish peoples, 76–77
salty taste, 106
Saluki, 85, 110
Samoyed, 181
Sascha (dog), 119–20
Savolainen, Peter, 43–44, 57
scavengers, 47–49, 53
scent, 107–9, 132–33
scent dogs, 133
scent hounds, 68
scent-marking, 133
schnauzer, 111, 181, 185
*Science* (magazine), 43, 44
Scott, John Paul, 91–92, 93, 95,
    97
Scottish deerhound, 68
Scottish terrier, 181
sea lions, 10
seals, 10, 75
Seaman (dog), 81
Seaman's Creek, 81
Seeing Eye organization, 84
selective pressure, 114
self, sense of, 161–62
self-awareness, 137, 148, 149, 151,
    158–60
self-consciousness, 162–63
senses, 101–21. *See also specific senses*
sensitive period, 96–97
Serengeti, 199
setters, 79
sexual behavior, inappropriate, 98
sexual maturity, 37, 98